MW01031724

"This is the best book on endu this book was going to be different—Trillia Newbell has given us something that is deeply wise, practical at every turn, and laden with illuminating illustrations. Again and again she points us to Jesus and reminds us each time that the hope for our endurance is not found in our faithfulness but rather made possible because of his. You don't have to dread the race ahead; you can look at the road ahead with anticipation and hope. This book will tell you why."

Paul David Tripp, pastor and author of *New Morning Mercies*

"The longer I live, the more I want to finish the Christian race well and hear the words, 'Well done, good and faithful servant.' Trillia Newbell's newest book, *Sacred Endurance*, offers practical and personal encouragement to faithfully live the Christian life, daily looking to Jesus. Amid life's hardships and struggles, her words will refresh your soul and spur you on in the race."

Melissa Kruger, director of women's content at The Gospel Coalition, author of *In All Things*

"If you're reading this, you're breathing. And if you're breathing that can only mean one thing—God isn't finished with you yet! No matter the premature judgments of others, your race is not over! *Sacred Endurance* is just the oxygen we need to help us hear those two words from our Father we long for, 'Well Done!'"

Bryan Loritts, lead pastor, Abundant Life Christian Fellowship, author of *Insider/Outsider*

"As a friend and colleague of Trillia Newbell, I can testify that the author lives out the message of this book every day. She is characterized by joy, exuberance, and persistence. Maybe you, like me, are sometimes finding yourself feeling exhausted by the whirl of life all around us. This book will equip you to keep running, with your feet on the ground and your eyes on the prize."

Russell Moore, president, the Ethics and Religious Liberty Commission of the Southern Baptist Convention

"Trillia refreshingly highlights stories of enduring faith in a relatable, vulnerable tone. I leave this book more convinced that Jesus is the true hero of every enduring saint."

Quina Aragon, author of *Love Made: A Story of God's Overflowing, Creative Heart*

"If you've never felt like giving up on the Christian race, this book is not for you. If you've never doubted whether your faith is strong enough to last, this book is not for you. If you're confident that you've 'got this'—this book is definitely not for you. If, however, you know your own weakness, if you feel the weight of the world dragging you down, if you cry out 'Lord, I believe! Help my unbelief!'—then *Sacred Endurance* may just be the hope and help you need to keep running. With honesty and compassion, author Trillia Newbell urges us on, reminding us to trust, not in ourselves but in the kindness and mercy of Christ."

Hannah Anderson, author of *Humble Roots: How Humility Grounds and Nourishes Your Soul*

"Incredibly timely; accessible and warm. *Sacred Endurance* reminds us of the burden, blessedness, strategy, and assurance of this 'race' in Jesus Christ. On fire for God or are you a dimly lit wick? I guess the answer depends on what day it is for some of us. This book will meet you where you are, and I believe it will re-offer you the promises found in Scripture, fueling faith as we journey with Jesus and call after those who seem to be slipping away."

Christina H. Edmondson, dean for intercultural student development at Calvin College, cohost, Truth's Table podcast

"We live during in a time in history when having spotty Wi-Fi or slower than split-second downloads results in irritation and complaints. We are used to microwaves reheating our food in under a minute and news content delivered in 280 characters over Twitter. Trillia's book *Sacred Endurance* invites the reader to step back and take a long-haul look at the Christian life. Both the whys and hows are covered as she explores what it looks like to have a lasting faith that ends in our ultimate prize of being face to face with our King. She sums up well our purpose on earth, 'This is our sacred endurance: running the race of the Christian life set before us by the grace of God, through the strength of God, until the day we face our God.'"

Vivian Mabuni, speaker and author of *Open Hands, Willing Heart: Discover the Joy of Saying Yes to God*

"*Sacred Endurance* is a rich biblical exploration of our call to persevere. Practical, gospel-centered, and serious, Trillia's book helps readers to run faithfully without denying or downplaying the reality of suffering and evil we face in this life."

Alan Noble, assistant professor of English at Oklahoma Baptist University, author of *Disruptive Witness*

SACRED ENDURANCE

FINDING GRACE AND STRENGTH
FOR A LASTING FAITH

TRILLIA J. NEWBELL

An imprint of InterVarsity Press
Downers Grove, Illinois

InterVarsity Press
P.O. Box 1400, Downers Grove, IL 60515-1426
ivpress.com
email@ivpress.com

InterVarsity Press® is the book-publishing division of InterVarsity Christian Fellowship/USA®, a movement of students and faculty active on campus at hundreds of universities, colleges, and schools of nursing in the United States of America, and a member movement of the International Fellowship of Evangelical Students. For information about local and regional activities, visit intervarsity.org.

Scripture quotations, unless otherwise noted, are from The Holy Bible, English Standard Version, copyright © 2001 by Crossway Bibles, a division of Good News Publishers. Used by permission. All rights reserved.

While any stories in this book are true, some names and identifying information may have been changed to protect the privacy of individuals.

Cover design and image composite: David Fassett
Interior design: Daniel van Loon
Images: outdoor staircase: © Thanwa Chulajata / EyeEm / Getty Images
      plants: © Sofya Moskalenko / EyeEm / Getty Images
      roots: © Kladuk / iStock / Getty Images Plus

ISBN 978-0-8308-4578-1 (print)
ISBN 978-0-8308-4838-6 (digital)

Printed in the United States of America ♾

InterVarsity Press is committed to ecological stewardship and to the conservation of natural resources in all our operations. This book was printed using sustainably sourced paper.

Library of Congress Cataloging-in-Publication Data

A catalog record for this book is available from the Library of Congress.

P   25   24   23   22   21   20   19   18   17   16   15   14   13   12   11   10   9   8   7   6   5   4   3   2   1

Y   39   38   37   36   35   34   33   32   31   30   29   28   27   26   25   24   23   22   21   20   19

To Thern,

my husband, my friend,

my fellow sojourner

running the race set before us,

hoping in Jesus and

fixing our eyes on him—

together.

He is with us till the end and then forevermore.

CONTENTS

CALLED TO A RACE

I press on toward the goal for the prize of the
upward call of God in Christ Jesus.

PHILIPPIANS 3:14

On August 28, 1963, Mahalia Jackson took to the stage to use her beautiful, soulful voice to encourage the souls of more than a quarter million men and women gathered at the Lincoln Memorial for the March on Washington, organized to advocate for the civil and economic rights of African Americans.

Jackson endured many trials as she got involved in the civil rights movement by singing and providing financial support. As her gospel music gained widespread popularity, she received death threats from neighbors in her quiet Chicago neighborhood. During that day on the Lincoln Memorial, she would be instrumental in the creation of Martin Luther King Jr.'s most famous speech, "I Have a Dream." She reportedly called out from behind him on the podium, "Tell 'em about the dream, Martin. Tell 'em about the dream!" That urging led him to ditch his notes and use the refrain, "I have a dream."

Jackson's place in history, including but not limited to gospel music and the civil rights movement, is remarkable yet not widely known. She was devoted to living out the gospel and singing God's praises. And on that day, she belted out two songs. The first, "How I Got Over," is a song of endurance in the face of hardship, and the lyrics describe her own hard times. How did she "get over"? She looked to Jesus, the one who died and suffered for her. She sang this in recognition of her Savior:

And I want to thank him for how he brought me . . .
Oh thank my God how he kept me.
I'm gonna thank him 'cause he never left me.[1]

After a life of miserable trials and wonderful mercies, Jackson finished her race in January 1972 at the age of sixty.[2]

RUNNING YOUR RACE

You also are in a race for your life. That may surprise you as you sit in a comfy chair or lounge in a coffee shop reading this book, but it's true. It's a race that requires all of you, and it's not easy. Jackson was in a race for her life, and the lyrics she sang to that large crowd reminded them that they too were in a race. She sang in wonder of how she'd made it through all those years of struggling and falling. And then she gave the answer, the same answer that will get you and me over.

You may not face the struggles of segregation and threats of lynching, but you too will have to endure. You'll struggle along the way. You likely have already.

One of the biggest lies about the Christian faith is that it should be easy. But God doesn't give us that promise. He never said we would be without trouble. Things threaten to trip us up in our race: someone we love dishonors the marriage bed and finds another person; God seems to prosper those who've wronged us. Doubts come into our heads, and we wonder if God's Word is true. Does God mean what he says? When life seems dull and things other than God bring greater joy and pleasure—at least momentarily—we find we're no longer attending church, let alone thinking about God.

You and I are in a race.

Over the past few years, I've seen marriages of friends fall apart. I've talked with parents whose teenage son no longer believes in God. I've seen churches almost split, and I've walked through broken relationships.

And then there's the everyday ups and downs of life. Sometimes the race feels almost effortless, as if you could continue indefinitely with a tailwind at your back, carrying you forward. But other times you're hardly moving or even incapable of taking another step.

In the American context, it's easy to be comfortable with our faith. We can be culturally good but spiritually dead. But there's a reason the Bible often refers to the Christian life as a race. There is much at stake, and getting to the end takes more trust and effort than we'd like to admit. Our integrity, our witness, and even our very lives are at stake.

And there's grace available for every single step we take, every act of faith, every decision to obey. Every single thing we do is covered and shored up by the grace of God. Thankfully, the prize at the end of this race couldn't be more worth our pressing on in the struggle.

I want to share a story with you, a story about a race I ran. You may have a similar sort of memory about athletic endeavors or one about a mental struggle. It can remind you about life and faith and about discovering what it means to run well for God's glory.

It was a race of a lifetime—at least that's how it felt to this seventeen-year-old in the anchor leg of the 4x400 relay on the biggest stage in my state. I was the team's anchor, so the relay ended with me. I would build on the efforts of my teammates, and the result would post when I crossed the line. As my turn came, it felt like everything was riding on me. Could I maintain the incredible pace all the way around the track without my body giving out? I'd practiced innumerable times and knew how to pace myself, but as my team was in first place (leading one of the fastest teams in the state), adrenaline and nerves took over.

As I waited for my teammate to complete her lap, the sun beat down on my head, and sweat dripped off my chin. The third runner on the team rounded the last curve and headed down the straightaway to hand off the baton to me. When she was within twenty meters, I started to run, reaching back like we'd practiced countless times before to secure the baton and officially begin my leg of the race. Baton in hand, my brain sent one simple, screaming message: run!

I took off—sprinting as fast as I ever had. My legs began moving at a speed I'd never experienced. I rounded the first curve and still had plenty of energy left. I completed the back stretch, feeling strong. Then I completed the final turn successfully. But with just one hundred meters left, something happened. My legs began to give out. The ability to lift my feet and put them back down quickly had greatly diminished.

I felt like I was running in mud. Every stride took maximum effort. I could feel myself slowing down—after the way I'd started, it was like slow motion—but I wasn't quitting. The crowd was up on its feet, screaming and pointing. I had maintained a good lead through three hundred meters, but now another racer was on my heels, catching up. With each step closer to the finish line, I experienced great relief and great pain.

I was so close. . . . Would I make it to the end? I could taste it. I could see it. Would I get the prize that my team sought?

Yes! I crossed the finish line and collapsed. I was exhausted, but we were state champions. When I think about that race, even now my breath leaves me. And I can't help but grin. I can't believe I finished that race. Had I known what lay ahead of me, I'm not sure I would have taken the starting line. But the excruciating strain of the last hundred meters was worth the joy of winning with my team.

GOD'S PROVISION IN THE RACE

Similarly we're called to a spiritual race, a sacred race, and God will supply all we need for that race. "The race that is set before us" is the Christian life (Heb 12:1-2). More specifically our race set before us is our hope in Jesus as we hold fast to our confession, trusting in the One who is faithful (Heb 6:18; 10:23). Our hope is that we get to the end of our days, saying, "I have fought the good fight, I have finished the race, I have kept the faith" (2 Tim 4:7). That's our end goal. That's our finish line. And we look forward to rewards at the end of this great race.

Like my track meet, the Christian life is a race that will have an end. One day we'll be complete in glory and with Christ. We'll receive a prize when this race is finished. But until that time, we must learn to run, endure, persevere, and finish.

The race of faith isn't easy; it takes effort—sometimes significant effort, a finishing-the-final-hundred-meters type of effort. It has great joys but can also be painful. We can fall and will definitely struggle, so there are moments when it's tempting to quit. This is why we need to learn how to condition our mind, soul, and body for the race set before us.

The Scriptures are filled with stories of saints who endured to the end while stumbling along the way. If they weren't stumbling because of their sin, they were being tossed about by the trials of life. My mind often turns to the apostle Paul, who endured imprisonment and beatings and ridicule and betrayal—all for Jesus. What motivated him to stay in the race? Maybe it was the prize. As we see in Philippians 3:14, it was also because he was called to the race, and he understood his calling.

Before we look directly at that text, let's take a look at the Scriptures before it. Paul was warning the Philippian church to watch out for those who would attribute progress toward godliness to works of the law and who would place their confidence and security in themselves. On the contrary, you and I are to "put no confidence in the flesh" (Phil 3:3). Paul then went on to share why he could have confidence in the flesh had he chosen to; his pedigree as a Pharisee and a persecutor of the church was a badge of honor in the first century (Phil 3:4-7). But he wrote that he counted it all as rubbish; it was trash compared to what he'd gained in knowing and being found in Christ (Phil 3:8-10). Paul would do anything to become like his Savior and to obtain the prize of being with Christ for eternity (Phil 3:11).

Paul hadn't yet obtained this great gift, but he was willing to suffer, to deny himself, and to die in the name of Jesus as he waited to obtain it. He was motivated. He had a clear goal and vision. He knew that the path toward that goal was filled with obstacles and was worth it. He pressed on toward the goal for the "prize of the upward call of God in Christ Jesus" (Phil 3:14).

In the pages ahead, you and I will be thinking a lot about the race and how we finish it. And it's good for us to consider that we're called to this race. When my coach invited me to run that track event, my status as an individual athlete was transformed. I was no longer representing myself; I was representing the school and the team. It was bigger than me. In the same way, God, in his mercy and kindness, has given us a calling that trumps all earthly calls: we have a "heavenly calling" (Heb 3:1). Knowing that we are not our own and that we are called to this race by a gracious God who helps us run it—not only as his children but also as his ambassadors—helps us run with endurance.

When I was finishing the 4x400, had it been all about me, I would have given up. But knowing that it wasn't just about me helped me push through the pain. Similarly this race of faith I'm running isn't all about me—it's about Jesus. Remembering that Jesus is the author and perfecter of my faith, knowing that I'm an ambassador to the living God, and remembering that I will gain more of him keeps me focused properly on this race. You and I have been called to run, but it's not all about us. It's all about him who called us.

NOT AN EASY CALL

I thoroughly enjoy health and athletics. I've spent most of my life either doing a sport or teaching others about fitness. In my adulthood, fitness hasn't been just a hobby for me; at one time it was a career path. I taught group fitness classes, trained fitness instructors, and even owned a small fitness studio. Though I no longer do fitness professionally, it continues to be an important part of who I am.

Here's the thing I've learned about fitness: it takes time, effort, patience, falling on your face in agony at times, and lots and lots of enduring. You don't wake up one day, decide to run a marathon, and then run it that evening. You have to train your body and mind for months. You have to endure difficult workouts, setbacks, and the daily routine required. Even then, getting to the finish line may be a slow process. And some quit.

This is what it's like to run the Christian race as well. We learn how to work the muscles of godly pursuits that result in sanctification; this is our sacred endurance. I'm motivated as a believer not because I have to but because I get to. Yet obstacles, real-life struggles, hard circumstances, and ordinary life make running the life of faith difficult. I've had my fair share of difficulties, including the death of my father and sister, four miscarriages, and a number of other painful experiences and circumstances—from health scares to broken relationships. Church life hasn't always been sunshine and rainbows, especially because I'm part of an ethnic minority. During a season of bitterness, repentance seemed a daily duty, and relief seemed far away.

All this to say, it won't be easy. But you and I have been called to endure, to walk worthily, and to be imitators of Christ. And we're compelled to continue the race because of the saving work that Jesus has accomplished for us, independent of any efforts of our own.

One difference between a track-and-field race and the Christian race is that in the second we don't finish in our own strength. We don't have to find every muscle fiber in our body and practice "mind over matter" to finish. Instead we have great promises in the Word of God that help us realize that he is running this race with us and that the Holy Spirit is at work within us to equip us and empower us in the race. God has ultimate control, and holding onto that reality can bring us rest and peace.

Our strength and abilities don't come through our own doing; you and I are equipped and strengthened by the Lord. Too often, however, this life of faith is confusing as we think through our circumstances and as we fight our personal battles with sin and temptation. How do these two fit together: are we truly saved by grace, or do we have to work really hard? Perhaps it seems you must earn your salvation and that the prize at the finish line depends completely on your own effort. Or maybe you've given up. Instead of running that difficult stretch, you collapsed and decided it was simply too hard, too painful, or too discouraging.

Maybe you've tried and tried, and now that you've tasted grace, you think the best way to finish the race is simply to run the race however you want. So instead of running the circle of the track, you're going to run zigzags, just because you can. Yes, you're free to do that, even if those zigzags aren't what the Master intended. Some leave the track entirely and pursue a different destination.

SO, WHAT DO YOU DO NOW?

How do you endure in fighting sin with faith? How exactly do you fight temptations? Do you even have endurance? Is it possible to work hard in fighting temptation and sin without becoming prideful and falling into the mindset that your salvation is based on your efforts rather than on grace? Is it better to throw up your hands in what feels like a pointless fight against sin and relish the unconditional love and grace of God?

Thankfully we're able to go to the Word of God and sort out some of this confusion. But some questions of this life won't be fully answered until we are with our Savior. Because God's Word has plenty to say, my hope and prayer is that by the end of this book, you and I will have a better understanding of how to finish the race and finish it well.

I'm not at the end of my race. I'm in my forties with a preteen and a teen to continue to raise, and I've been married for less than two decades. So I'm in the middle of my race, and I'm learning what it means to keep running. I pray that *Sacred Endurance* will be a means of grace to help you and me along the path.

In this book, I explore the importance of enduring, the grace available to us, the challenges we face, the pursuit of godliness, and the prize you and I can look forward to. You'll read stories about the Christian life—sometimes successes, sometimes struggles—and about endurance and motivation to push on toward Jesus.

God commands us to walk in a manner worthy of our calling. And he says that he will finish the good work he began in us (Phil 1:6). He who called us is faithful, and "he will surely do it" (1 Thess 5:24). Our life is a fight of faith, and we'll explore how to exercise spiritually for it. We'll look at some of the character traits—such as perseverance, faithfulness, patience, sacrifice, and even risk—that are developed in us as we walk.

Let me also share what *Sacred Endurance* is *not* about. This book is not about theological debates on assurance or perseverance; it's not about whether or not you can lose your salvation. I will not try to convince you to believe a certain doctrine. Instead I'll work under the assumption that we will endure to the end. Enduring to the end doesn't mean not failing (and by failing, I mean failing miserably); it means that when we come to our end, we're still believing and trusting in the finished work of Jesus Christ on our behalf. We're still repentant and resting in him. Let's assume that if we've truly placed our faith and trust in the work of Jesus Christ, our salvation is secure.

Sacred Endurance helps us peek under the curtain of real-life struggles while running the race set before us. There are reasons people don't endure to the end. What are they? Some theologians suggest that if a person doesn't endure to the end, he or she was never a believer. Maybe. But we want to prepare for the reasons that make it simply hard to live, and we want to be able to say that out loud without shame. I hope we'll see that we aren't alone in the struggle and that we can endure by God's grace.

THE BOTTOM LINE

So, what is the assumption we're working under as we think through enduring? I adopt the view laid out in the biblical theology book *The Race Set Before Us* by Thomas Schreiner and Ardel Caneday. Consider this promise in Scripture: "And I am sure of this, that he who began a good work in you will bring it to completion at the day of Jesus Christ" (Phil 1:6). Likewise consider this warning: "Note then the kindness and the severity of God: severity toward those who have fallen, but God's kindness to you, provided you continue in his kindness. Otherwise you too will be cut off" (Rom 11:22). For some, these seem to contradict one another. So is God going to keep me in the end, or am I going to be cut off? There are varying views, but the view I will be working from believes this:

> God's promises have their own function, namely, to establish belief in God who keeps his promises and to assure us that he is faithful to his people. . . . God's warnings and admonitions have their distinctive function. They serve to elicit belief that perseveres in faithfulness to God's heavenly call on us. . . . The warnings serve the promises, for the warnings urge belief and confidence in God's promises.[3]

In other words, the warnings and admonitions call for faith that endures to receive the prize. God will keep us to the end, and the warnings and admonitions in the Scriptures help guide us toward that end. God's strength and his enduring faithfulness will enable us to get there. He has given us his Word as a means of grace and instruction. And he has given us his Spirit to help and equip.

What a gracious God! This is our sacred endurance: running the race of the Christian life set before us by the grace of God, through the strength of God, until the day we face our God.

JESUS AND THE CLOUD OF WITNESSES

Therefore, since we are surrounded by so great a cloud of witnesses,
let us also lay aside every weight, and sin which clings so closely,
and let us run with endurance the race that is set before us,
looking to Jesus, the founder and perfecter of our faith, who for
the joy that was set before him endured the cross, despising the
shame, and is seated at the right hand of the throne of God.

HEBREWS 12:1-2

My relay race could have ended in disaster. I was at the end of my rope. My legs were giving out. I was done. But I was running not only for myself but also for others. It wasn't just about me; I wasn't pushing to the finish line alone.

The crowd was up on its feet. My beloved father was yelling, "Go, Trillia, go!" My coach was running along the sidelines as if he could be my legs and feet, pushing me along with his cheers and warnings: "You've got this! She's right behind you, but keep your focus ahead. Go!" Everyone was screaming. And this is no exaggeration. I can almost feel it now. It was intense—and intensely motivating! I had a cloud of witnesses cheering me on.

I could see those who cheered me onto the finish line, and I could hear them. Although we don't see them or hear them, we all have a heavenly "cloud of witnesses" who have gone before us and who are cheering us on to the finish line. God is so generous that he has given us a description of these witnesses in Hebrews 12:1. So who are these witnesses, and what is their function? Well, it depends on who you ask.

The *therefore* in this verse gives us a clue to look at the chapter behind. In Hebrews 11, the writer laid out the faithfulness of Old Testament saints who endured hardship, worked through fear, suffered—and finished the race well. Our cloud of witnesses includes but is not limited to these:

- Enoch, who walked with God and believed in him (Heb 11:5; Gen 5:21-24)

- Noah, who trusted God with the unknown and obeyed him (Heb 11:7; Gen 6:9–9:29)

- Abraham, who obeyed when he didn't know what would happen (Heb 11:8-10; Gen 12:1-4; Heb 11:17-19; Gen 22:1-19)

- Sarah, who doubted at first but then trusted when her circumstances seemed impossible (Heb 11:11-12; Gen 21:1-7)

- Moses, who chose a path of suffering and ridicule rather than wealth and power (Heb 11:24; Ex. 2:11-15)

- Rahab, who did not perish with those who were disobedient (Heb 11:31; Josh 6:25)

The noun *witnesses* (Greek *martyrōn*, Heb 12:1) means both "those who see" and "those who say."[1] These people have seen or been a witness to something, and they testify about it. In

Hebrews 11, the cloud of witnesses saw the faithfulness of God and proclaimed it through their lives. *Witness* can also mean "one who watches." In Hebrews 12:1 the idea that the cloud of witnesses is surrounding us gives a picture of us being watched.[2]

Some theologians, such as Henry Alford, believe without a doubt that all the saints before us are peering down to cheer us on. Others hold a more open interpretation.[3] I tend to believe that it's a mystery, but the Lord used words like *surrounded* and *clouds* to indicate a place and time. Right now we're surrounded by a cloud of witnesses.

This faithful cloud of witnesses has continued to grow and includes people you may even know personally. What a glorious thought! My hope for you and me is that we too would join such a cloud.

In first-century Greece, sporting events in arenas were a common source of entertainment. Just as a crowd means something to us, it also meant something to the readers of the author's letter to the Hebrews.[4] As during an arena event, there's a cloud cheering and spurring us on. They've gone before us and are screaming, as my coach did, "Keep your focus ahead. Go!" They don't intercede for us—only Christ does—but the thought of believers just like us going before us should be an encouragement as we walk.

The word *witness* may have also meant that they are examples of faithfulness. They witness to us by their lives. They are a cloud that has gone before us, and we can look to their faithfulness as we seek to finish this race. The word translated as *race* in Hebrews 12:1 is *agōna*, which is an agonizing struggle or contest. The Christian walk is not a cakewalk, so we look to people like Abraham and Moses and Sarah and Rahab, who understood the struggle of faith and endured to the end.

Why the need for a cheering squad? Why the need for examples of faithfulness? Because the weight of sin that burdens us can slow our pace, cause us to stumble, and prevent us from making it to the end in one piece. Some things cling closely to us that hinder our walk and cloud our view such as the consequences of sin.

LAYING SIN ASIDE

One of the significant challenges in this race we run as Christians is the tension of being saved by grace alone and of being called into a new, challenging life. This life is to be marked by endurance in pursuing Christ, modeling our lives after his perfect example, even as we know that this side of heaven we fall far short. You and I need to work toward understanding why we run this race, what we're running for, and the tensions we must navigate along the way.

Since we have this cloud of witnesses, we "lay aside every weight, and sins which cling so closely" (Heb 12:1). The cloud of witnesses is one motivator to lay aside every weight. *But what is the weight?*

Have you ever watched a cycling road race, swim meet, or track-and-field event? If you have, you've likely noticed one thing: the athletes aren't wearing much, and if they are, it's skin-tight. There's good reason for this: these sports, when executed competitively, require a minimal amount of interference. Swimmers need to be able to glide through water. Cyclists want to minimize wind resistance, and runners can't be weighed down.

Similarly we need to get rid of everything that would hinder our walk. Every weight must go. That sounds strong because it is. It may even sound legalistic—but it isn't. If something encumbers our walk, we need to figure out a way to adjust it or to lay it aside.

In Genesis 3, it's clear Adam and Eve made a mess of our lives and of the world. Their fall created the need for us to endure. Without their fall, life wouldn't require enduring, persevering, struggling, agonizing, and the like. But now we must fight not only the elements and various circumstances that come our way but also our sin nature. Although we who place our faith and trust in the finished work of Jesus are new creations, we still seek to put off our old self, to fight sin, and to resist the pull of temptation (Eph 4:22).

If anyone says he is without sin, he is a liar (1 Jn 1:8). God said that, and I'm just repeating it—so don't blame the messenger! The struggle is real, and the struggle is hard. The struggle can also lead to destruction if we don't fight. As the apostle Paul wrote, "Now that you have been set free from sin and have become slaves of God, the fruit you get leads to sanctification and its end, eternal life. For the wages of sin is death, but the free gift of God is eternal life in Christ Jesus our Lord" (Rom 6:22-23).

We have been set free from sin, but there are times when the allure of sin seems too strong. This reminds me of my own fight. Recently I was diagnosed with a hiatal hernia. A small opening in the top of my stomach allows acid to get into my abdomen, and part of my stomach pushes up through my diaphragm muscle. Yes, it's just as painful as it sounds. Some

people with the condition require surgery, but I've
I can control the side effects with a healthy diet.
diet is beyond healthy. I need to cut out even good-for-you
grains and carbohydrates to prevent upsetting my system.

The trouble is, all those foods that I must deny myself in
order to control my condition are *so* delicious. More times than
I'd like to admit, I've indulged in something that I knew be-
forehand wouldn't be good for me. In those moments, my ap-
petite was met and my taste buds were satisfied. But just as the
food settled in my stomach, the cramps, coughing, and overwhelming sense of nausea returned. It happens almost every
time I lack the self-control to say no. There are consequences
for my actions, and if I am not careful, the result could lead to
greater health problems—and even death.

My desire for food that I shouldn't eat reminds me of the allure
of sin. At times I can clearly see the ugliness of sin and its deceitful nature. But then there are times when I ignore the Spirit's
prompting and warnings, and I give in to the flesh. Sin can lie to
our hearts and minds, telling us that it will be satisfying.

Think about the last time you were angry with someone and
either gave her the cold shoulder or spit out a sharp comeback.
The response may have felt satisfying at the time, but "a soft
answer turns away wrath" (Prov 15:1). Or what about that
time you took a quick glance at that forbidden website, only
to find yourself swallowed up in its false and grotesque por-
trayal of intimacy. Misery and shame followed. We can no
doubt think of a number of things we do that we ought not to
do. And the long-term results can be devastating. Instant
gratification is just that, instant. It quickly dissipates. Lasting

enjoyment, however, comes from denying self, rejecting sin, and pursuing Jesus.

OUR ESCAPE ROUTE

God's Word doesn't make light of our sin. We see in Romans 6:23 that the result of—or the punishment for—sin is death. Sin kills the body and the soul. Sin corrupts everything. When sin came into the world, it brought death and darkness, brokenness and shame. And when we deliberately sin, when we give in to the desires of our flesh, we are saying yes to death.

But God has provided a way of escape: "No temptation has overtaken you that is not common to man. God is faithful, and he will not let you be tempted beyond your ability, but with the temptation he will also provide the way of escape, that you may be able to endure it" (1 Cor 10:13). We can say no to sin by the power of the Holy Spirit and the grace of God. We have been set free from sin and are no longer ruled by its power (Rom 6:22).

This doesn't mean we don't sin and we won't sin. We will sin and we do sin. When we want to do good, evil is right there with us (Rom 7:21). But when we have a choice—a clear choice—we've been given the power to say no. What freedom! That's a reason for rejoicing!

It's true that the wages of sin is death. And to pay for our sin requires death—the death of the perfect Son of God, Jesus Christ. Jesus died the death we deserve. He paid the penalty we earned. Jesus is the reason for our freedom, the giver of the free gift that leads to eternal life (Rom 6:23). This is most definitely reason for more rejoicing! Jesus paid for a debt we could never pay on our own; it was far too great to pay. We now have freedom and receive grace. Let's take that freedom and live in a way that's worthy of this awesome gospel. We can't do it on our own, and that's why God gives himself more and more, so we can have the power to be slaves of God.

As we put off the sin that clings so closely, we become more and more like our Savior. This is the story of grace. We sin and we sin again, but Jesus died for all of our sins, so we're freed from the power of sin. We're given all the things necessary to be more like him. As those who have been set free from the chains of sin, we are being sanctified—made more like Christ. We're being transformed from one degree of glory to the next (2 Cor 3:18).

So the next time you're tempted by sin, remember this free gift. We don't obey because it earns us favor. Favor is already ours. It has been bought with a price. So instead we obey because we love Jesus and are compelled toward obedience by his love. Perhaps that's why the writer of Hebrews urged his readers to look to Jesus in the race.

IT'S ALREADY DONE

The knowledge of our sin can be overwhelming if there isn't also the understanding of God's amazing grace toward us. Condemnation hinders our pursuit of godliness, so before I move on to right theology and running the race, let me remind you to be encouraged in your faith. My hope is that we start every day reminding ourselves of this truth of the gospel: we are all saved by grace and not by our works. This is a free gift to each one of us, and we need to keep this gospel truth as our firm foundation.

We need not fear the rejection of our Father—ever. We don't need to suffer under the weight of our own judgment of ourselves when Jesus paid it all. Who are we to do that? We get to instead enjoy Jesus, live free of the guilt of sin, repent when we do sin, and ask God for the strength to walk in a manner worthy of the gospel. We take our eyes off ourselves and our performance and fix them on the One who did what we could never do on our own. Rest in him. Worship and rejoice—for your sins are forgiven! Thankfully God didn't leave any part of our salvation up to us. Jesus truly is our Savior.

I recently came upon a sermon that speaks clearly about this great accomplishment of Jesus on our behalf. Read (and then reread!) these words of Elder D. J. Ward:

> Now, I hear this on television and I hear it in churches, that God has done all he can do. The rest is up to you. If the rest is up to you, then he didn't accomplish it. If anything is up to you, he didn't accomplish it.
>
> I've even heard this: you've got to help God save you. He can't do it by himself. If God cannot do it by himself, then he didn't accomplish it. He's a false god. He's a liar and you best not trust him. If he didn't do it, then we ought to stop singing "Jesus paid it all." Sing, "He paid some of it."
>
> Now brothers and sisters, if he did not accomplish it, we are here in vain. And you can have all the religion you want, if this was not accomplished, we are going to hell. It's just that blunt, it's just that simple, it's just that clear.

But if he did do it, he doesn't need your best and your works need not speak for you. If he did do it, you can leave here rejoicing that your sins are now under the blood. And he stands as your substitute, your mediator before God this morning.

I declare this morning he paid it all! He paid it all. Every drop of it. Every sin I was going to commit. Every sin I thought about committing. He nailed it to his cross and I bear it no more! Praise the Lord! Praise the Lord![5]

You are loved because of Jesus. And this is good news. Jesus paid it all!

You and I can't even think about enduring in the faith without grabbing hold of this glorious truth as we pursue the Lord and the transforming power of his Spirit. This pursuit is not for our own glory and honor but because we are compelled by Christ and what he has done. With our salvation secure through the work of Christ and the grace extended to us as a result, you and I run this race amid a cloud of witnesses cheering us on toward a Savior waiting to give us the ultimate prize (Heb 12:1).

Let's explore together what it means to run this race well and receive the prize, to live a life that brings the Lord glory and takes us deep into more of him. This is a race you and I are blessed to run because we get to; we are compelled by the amazing love, grace, and sacrifice of Christ.

FOCUSING ON JESUS

As we put off the weight of sin, we firmly establish the object of our gaze. We must set our gaze and never look away. When a dancer first learns how to do a turn, she's encouraged to find a spot and, with each rotation, keep her eyes fixed on that spot. This allows her to turn without falling over or getting dizzy.

Similarly setting our gaze properly changes everything about our race. Although we're encouraged by the cloud of witnesses, we don't set our eyes on those who have gone before us because they are imperfect. They may be examples of faithfulness walked out, but only God is fully and perfectly faithful. Only Jesus is the founder and perfecter of our faith. He alone is to be worshiped. He is our perfect motivator. As Philip Hughes wrote in his commentary on Hebrews,

> What could be more necessary than to keep constantly before our eyes him who is the pioneer and perfecter of our faith? Apart from him in whom all the promises of God find their fulfillment, fallen mankind would have neither ground nor object of faith. It is on him, as we have seen, that in every age the gaze of faith is focused. He alone evokes and stimulates faith; and it is because he is the pioneer of our salvation (Heb 2:10) that he is the author of our faith.[6]

Jesus is the founder (in the Greek, the originator) of our faith. It all starts with him and all ends with him. He is the perfect mediator between God and us. He lived a perfect life. He died a sinner's death. There will never be a greater amount of suffering than what Jesus endured on the cross. Jesus, the perfect mediator, not only founded our faith, he will also see it all the way through. Yes, he is the perfecter of our faith. He will one day present us as holy and blameless (Col 1:22). Remarkable.

Hughes also wrote, "In looking to Jesus, then, we are looking to him who is the supreme exponent of faith, the one who, beyond all others, not only set out on the course of faith but also pursued it without wavering to the end. He, accordingly, is uniquely qualified to be the supplier and sustainer of the faith of his followers."[7]

Believing any of this even a little helps to motivate us in our race. Jesus has already done what we could never do. Our beautiful Savior continually invites us to come to him. In this race we cry out for help to fix our eyes on Jesus and to run to him. We desire to be singularly focused on the prize.

But who are we fooling? We know that even as we try to focus singularly on our Savior, we falter. We get distracted. We look to the left and right, and we go off course. Like a ballerina who looks slightly to her left in the midst of a spin, we tumble to the ground. We aren't going to do anything perfectly; that's one of many reasons we look to the one who is perfect. We aren't going to get things right every time, every day, and every moment of every day. We are going to struggle. Jesus was the perfect one, and we are not, so we look to him.

I drill this down in our hearts and minds because many try to run this race thinking they'll reach perfection one day, but they fall short and become disillusioned. They may walk away altogether. Sometimes the thing we need to throw off that hinders us isn't sin but condemnation. We'll explore other weights, but because sin clings so close to us, condemnation deserves the utmost attention. Jesus died for sins and the redemption of the world. This is his free gift of his grace.

I stress this because I know what it's like to run thinking I can earn God's favor and not resting in the life and work of Jesus on my behalf. Yes, even our good intentions can become clouded. We want to run, but we want to adjust our motives and not run as those trying to earn favor before God.

THE RIGHT MOTIVATIONS

The trashcan was full of CDs, and I was convinced it was for the best.

It was a small act, really, but one that was significant to this music-loving gal. Within a year or so after I became a Christian, I had thrown all of my CDs in the trash. I would have a fresh start and begin a new collection—one filled only with Christian music. After all, I was motivated by my love for and devotion to God. Having made my decision, I made sure others knew about my brave act of obedience so I would receive their approval.

The specifics of the trashed collection are forgotten now, I just knew that it felt more holy to throw them all away than to keep them. But was that action really motivated by a love for Jesus? No. I was more concerned about looking Christian than I was about being motivated by the gospel.

A music clean-out could certainly be a wise and God-honoring decision, but the motivation for such an action is vitally important. A friend once told me about a man who gave up baseball and then became legalistically transfixed on the idea that baseball was wrong—even to the point of becoming angry when someone invited him to a game. I guess we all have our things we do—things we believe will make God pleased with us.

Let's step back and recognize that the right motivations are essential for living consistently—that is, with our actions in step with our beliefs. When actions flow out of a heart that's motivated by the right reasons, we experience joy, freedom, gratitude, and peace. This is possible only if our motivations are rooted in Christ. It's also hard but incredibly freeing.

I had been motivated to *look* Christian, so throwing away all that music felt like the right decision to make, like what a good Christian ought to do. But my motivation didn't come out of a desire to guard against the temptation to indulge in the world; that music wasn't leading me to think sinful thoughts. So instead of joy, freedom, gratitude, and peace, I found guilt and dissatisfaction because of a desire to please others. I lacked the peace of knowing I was secure and loved in Christ.

JESUS' OBEDIENCE AND OURS

Any time we discuss running our race with endurance, it's good to make sure we're thinking rightly about our obedience and Jesus' obedience on our behalf. Jesus endured for the *joy* set before him (Heb 12:2)! His endurance was focused on joy.

Thankfully we have a Savior who relates to our suffering. Jesus is aware of and acquainted with the grief of humanity. He is acquainted with my grief and yours. The God-man endured trials and temptation but remained without sin (Heb 4:15). He was abandoned by his friends. He was a man of sorrows. He endured to the bitter end because he too was in a race. He was on a mission: the redemption of the world! The joy set before him was that he would be seated at the right hand of the Father. Death was defeated! So Jesus knows what it's like to endure; he understands what you experienced yesterday, what you will experience today, and what you will experience tomorrow.

On his way to the cross, Jesus sat and prayed to his Father, asking that if it was God's will, the cup of wrath would be taken away. Yet Jesus willingly drank that cup, and he hung on the cross. And in his final moments on the cross, he cried out, "My God, my God, why have you forsaken me?" (Mk 15:34).

His pain and suffering was for a purpose: the redemption of the world. He endured great pain—pain I can only imagine, pain and wrath on my behalf.[1] But he knew the end. And his endurance through pain and mocking—a death fit for a criminal, not a savior—was all because he was fulfilling a plan formed before the foundation of the world. And now we know that "we have such a high priest, one who is seated at the right hand of the throne of the Majesty in heaven" (Heb 8:1).

HAVING RIGHT MOTIVATIONS

As Christians, you and I want God's truth to inform how we think and how we live. We pray for the alignment of what is true, what we believe, what we think, and how we act. As we seek to live this out, we fight an important battle for the right motivations, and we resist wrong motivations. It's easy for our motivations to shift, so it's essential to root ourselves in the truth of the gospel continually: Christ sought you and me out while we were still sinners, and he humbled himself to take the punishment we deserve in order to give us new life to the glory of God. Jesus defeated death and promises to finish the work he began in us. This truth is the foundation of right motivations.

Your heart motivations matter because our God isn't fooled by outward appearance and actions. Running with the wrong motivations also leaves us depleted and wanting to give up this race. He desires our obedience both externally and internally—in action and in thought. This is why Jesus warned the Pharisees that to look beautiful on the outside meant nothing if inside they were full of death, uncleanliness, and impurity (Mt 23:27). There's freedom, joy, and praise to our God in living with the right motivations. As we look into our motivations, you and I need to recognize that we live a difficult tension as Christians: we are saved by grace and are compelled to put off the old self and walk in a way worthy of our calling.

What I was struggling with regarding CDs has a name: *legalism*. At its most basic, legalism is trying to save one's self. It's trying to do right things without believing that God justifies us by faith alone. It's trying to obey without God's help, without his power, and without his grace. Although legalism can look like trusting in God because of good works, it's actually a form of unbelief because we aren't resting in faith in the finished work of Jesus.

When we're motivated to work hard for God in order to earn his favor, we aren't operating with faith or trust. Instead we're trying to add to the finished work of Jesus on the cross. We're living as though his work isn't enough so we must strive to make him happy—as though our acceptance by God depends on our efforts.

Because we're justified through faith alone as a gift from God, you and I are freed from attempting to earn God's love and favor. Our salvation isn't—and never will be—a result of our works (Eph 2:8). There's nothing we could ever do to earn God's saving favor. No amount of sacrifice could earn us anything more. If you are in Christ, you have his favor—forever!

My temptation into legalism was motivated by selfish ambition. I was taking my works and showing them off to God. *Look, God! I threw out all my CDs for you.* This thought seems ridiculous now that it's written out. That's why Ephesians 2:9 is so important; salvation is "not a result of works, so that no one may boast." We don't finish the race and then boast in ourselves. That's what makes salvation a gift: it's free and unearned by us. So salvation isn't ultimately about you and me but about God. God does the work, and he receives the glory. A legalist wants to do the work, earn the favor, and get the glory.

It's probably apparent already that this isn't a good motivation because it's skewed and tainted by sin. Instead of pursuing good things out of the joy and knowledge of the firm standing and identity I have in Christ, my motivation was marked by insecurity, by selfishness, by mistrust, guilt, and doubt. We want to watch that our running toward Jesus isn't more about us and less about him.

I got this good advice from a pastor: "If you're struggling with legalism, don't fight it by quitting your Bible-reading time." In other words, if we aren't living out of the right motivations, there can be a temptation to jettison good things (such as Bible reading, acts of love, or evangelism) because we think they are part of the problem. Examining our motivations is a good thing; we need to be mindful about what's behind our actions. But in this process it's easy for confusion to set in.

In the midst of this confusion, look what has been revealed to us through God's Word:

- God has given us all we need for godliness (2 Pet 1:3).

- There is no condemnation for those in Christ Jesus (Rom 8:1).

- Our obedience to God comes out of our love for him (Jn 14:15).

If we struggle with legalism, somewhere in our pursuit of godliness we forget that only by God's grace can we live for him. God is the one who has granted us "all things that pertain to life and godliness" (2 Pet 1:3). In turn, his love motivates us. It is the fuel we need.

SO, WHAT'S *NOT* LEGALISM?

This is where confusion can set in. My desire to be careful about the music I listened to was a good thing. But when we equate the pursuit of godliness to legalism, we trade one significant problem for another. This mistake eventually leads to projecting judgment on others and even living licentiously. But as we saw earlier, we want to put off the sin, which clings so closely to us.

Pursuing godliness and practicing legalism are not the same. Though the actions may look similar, the motivation behind them is markedly different. Legalism comes out of self-centered motivations and a desire to earn God's favor, not obedience to God and radical love for others. The motivation you and I have as we live out our faith and pursue godliness comes through what has already been fully accomplished by Jesus and his free gift of saving grace.

This news is freeing. You and I can pursue Jesus, love Jesus, and learn about God as acts of faith-filled obedience. When we wake up in the morning and bow before God, it's an act of expressing our need for him. When we open our Bibles to hear his voice, we can do it not to procure his acceptance but to walk in fellowship with him.[2]

Unfortunately when we forget that any godliness and any sanctification we experience comes from our Father, we can become puffed up and begin to project our standards on others. Especially toxic is making moral standards out of priorities not described in Scripture. When we do this, we easily begin to judge and pressure people to conform to a lifestyle God never commanded. We forget about the good principles in the Bible that are foundational to our faith; instead we make our human practices the law.

It's human nature to distort God's glorious truths. While we may know what Scripture teaches about living as those who have been saved by grace through faith, we can forget. When we forget, our motivation becomes twisted. And that becomes a hindrance to godly living.

Admittedly it's tough to understand and balance the fact that our faith is through grace alone by faith alone *and* we are called to pursue good works to the glory of our Father. Living this out consistently and biblically is no small challenge. The grace that's unmerited favor with God is the same grace that teaches us to *renounce* (literally "disown") the ungodly ways of the world (Titus 2:11-12). Grace teaches us to discern and to separate ourselves from cultural sin but never to use ourselves as the standard.[3]

WATCH YOUR MOTIVES

Our motivation to fight against sin can never be to elevate ourselves. We aren't made to be worshiped and glorified, and gospel-centered motivation seeks to see our Father alone praised and glorified. So you and I must disown sin, starting with the sin in ourselves and then with the sins we see in culture, without becoming self-righteous in the process. This is a great tension of the Christian life; we are required to evaluate, examine, and ask the Lord to refine our motivations.

The world tells us to follow the motivations of our hearts—in other words, to do whatever we want. In contrast, Scripture gives us boundaries that aren't meant to stifle us but instead to help us to walk in the freedom of Christ. Legalism tells us that our motivation should be borne out of a desire to earn God's favor, while grace tells us we are free and can't earn the favor that has already been earned for us. Grace keeps us from holding unhealthy standards for ourselves and for others. It frees us from guilt, judgment, oppression, and the relentless daily grind of trying to fix ourselves. Endurance that lasts can come only out of motivation marked by grace, faith, love, and God's glory. Accompanied by the right motivations, living by grace sounds a lot like freedom, doesn't it?

Motivation that comes out of the grace you and I have received is life-giving. There is rest and peace and freedom in knowing that we're fully saved from our sin and that our Father in heaven couldn't love us any deeper.

This doesn't mean we can or should exploit the incredible grace we've been given. (See Romans 6.) The opposite is true: so moved and impacted by the free gift of grace, we're transformed and motivated to depths of love, worship, and devotion to Christ.

The author of the book of Hebrews wrote, "Let us hold fast the confession of our hope without wavering, for he who promised is faithful" (Heb 10:23). Have you ever had faith in something or someone that let you down? Whether it was a chair that didn't hold steady or a relationship that failed, we've all experienced times when we've put our trust or faith in something yet we were disappointed, hurt, or betrayed. And, as much as we may hate to admit it, we aren't just victims in this; we've let others down too.

But this is not your God. He has never let anyone down. He has never betrayed one of his promises. He has never been sorta trustworthy or pretty decent in follow-through for those who put their faith in him.

Our motivation comes out of our faith in a God who will never fail us. All others in our life might but not the Lord. To fail us would go against his very character. So to be motivated by faith is to be motivated by the very character and trustworthiness of God. There is no foundation as sure as him.

COMPELLED BY LOVE

Paul wrote to the church in Corinth about who they were in Christ, telling them to be motivated by love: "For Christ's love compels" (2 Cor 5:14 NIV). Think about what it means to be compelled. It isn't a drudgery or a dragging of feet. It isn't to be slightly encouraged or fairly interested in seeing the effect that something may have on your life.

No, to be compelled by the love of Christ is to be caught up and swept away. Envision a mountain river full to the brim with ice-cold rapids. Torrents of water race through the rocks, navigating turns, plunging ahead. Even if you just wade into this river, that's enough to catch you up and sweep you away. This is the effect of the love of Christ rightly understood.

To the heart that has been softened by the Holy Spirit, the love of Christ compels. It motivates. You and I are swept away by the extent of Christ's sacrifice, his pursuit of us, and by the new life he provides to those who are found in him.

Our world is full of messages telling us to live for our own glory, to seek to be noticed, to make a name for ourselves. As a society, we're caught up in the stories of individuals who achieve fame and prominence—whether they've worked hard to attain it or merely stumbled into it. The myriad of reality TV shows have a singular goal: make the winner famous by pushing her into the spotlight. If we aren't careful, the promise of instant fame draws our hearts. But our lives aren't meant to be lived for fame. You and I aren't made to glorify ourselves so that others will lift us up. We were made for the glory of God and God alone. How we live should be motivated by his glory, not our own.

We can refine our motivation by reflecting on who we are trying to glorify. Pursuing our own glory puts us on a path with no destination. There is no arrival point. And we're left unfulfilled and despairing. When we live for the glory of God, we find true joy and satisfaction in life. Our focus naturally shifts away from ourselves and to God. We can fight pride, jealousy, and comparison when our focus is not on our own glory but on God's.

Even in writing this, I realize that my motivations need to be refocused. It's easy to doubt that grace could cover all my sin. It's easy to feel that I could make God love me just a bit more if I did (or didn't do) certain things. It's easy to lose faith and begin to doubt God's character. It's easy to be compelled by the wrong things—even the pursuit of my own glory and prominence.

But instead we can:

Be motivated by the free gift that Jesus has given for you.

Be motivated by who God is.

Be motivated by what Jesus has done on your behalf.

Be motivated by the joy to be found in pointing praise, worship, and fame to the only one who deserves it.

Be motivated by Jesus, "the founder and perfecter of our faith, who for the joy that was set before him endured the cross, despising the shame, and is seated at the right hand of the throne of God" (Heb 12:2).

Be motivated by the fact that God has called you and that you have a prize waiting for you.

THE REAL CHRISTIAN LIFE

Beloved, do not be surprised at the fiery trial when it comes upon you to test you, as though something strange were happening to you. But rejoice insofar as you share Christ's sufferings, that you may also rejoice and be glad when his glory is revealed.

1 PETER 4:12-13

I remember when they got married. It was a glorious and beautiful summer day. Everyone looked their absolute best. It was nothing short of glamorous, which was my friend's style. Their first year of marriage brought the stereotypical fighting and wondering what happened to the sweetness of the honeymoon, but the years after were relatively calm and comfortable. Then came the kids—three wonderful, spunky kids, all two years apart from one another. Everything was standard and ordinary: school drop-offs and pickups, dinners, church on Sundays, and repeat.

But then the recession hit, and it hit hard. The husband's real estate business went upside down, and everything changed. Bills that were once barely thought of were now a strain to pay on time. The house was about to be foreclosed on. And the kids needed to be pulled from various activities. The financial strain and the disbelief that their lives were no longer comfortable brought out old wounds that were never discussed, and lively, unfiltered arguments became the new normal.

The husband slowly started to withdraw from his friends, and little by little he became more isolated. Eventually he found refuge in the arms of another woman. He walked away from the faith and his family. But the new relationship didn't last long.

This family hadn't prepared for the trials they may endure. They were also living a lie, with fake peace, not dealing with hurts along the way. The husband found that he had placed much of his identity in his work and money, so when that was taken away, he broke and ran away. He had everything that the American dream promises: a family, a good-paying job, status, and even church. But when everything fell apart, none of those things could sustain his faith.

THE DANGERS OF THE PROSPERITY GOSPEL

One reason those who profess faith in Christ run out of steam is that they were never told the truth about the Christian life. It isn't all dreary; there's much joy to be had, even in the midst of tough circumstances. But for many, Christianity means a get-out-of-bad-situations-free card. More seriously, this understanding of the faith has produced an entire health and/or wealth belief called the prosperity gospel. That "gospel" will not sustain you to the end.

The prosperity gospel purports that if the believer has enough faith, he or she will prosper in every way, and especially materially and financially. Most of this false gospel's leaders claim that if a person gives to their ministry, the donor will receive health and/or wealth in return.

Perhaps my statement that it's a *false* gospel seems too strong. But its claims are not only damaging to the person who hears them; they are indeed false. The true gospel never promises us health and wealth. Time and time again, the Scriptures remind us that following Christ means suffering and that there is joy and reward in our suffering (Jn 16:33; Rom 5:3-5; 8:18; 2 Tim 3:12; Jas 1:2-4; 1 Pet 5:10).

Many have been led astray through the prosperity gospel. Even if we don't fully believe in this teaching, aspects of our faith may be affected by it. It can manifest itself in the way we act, pray, and think. We can say or think things like this: "If I do this good thing, the Lord will bless me." "If I am perfectly pure, modest, and faithful, God will give me a spouse." "If I raise my kids a certain way, they will turn out perfect." In this thinking, everything is completely up to and about us. We think that our success and others', our joy, our circumstances, and all that God will or will not do is up to how we act, pray, or think.

But what happens when our circumstances are hard, when our finances are tight, when our children rebel, when our spouse cheats, when we become ill? Was it because we didn't have enough faith to believe? Was it because of some ill-advised plan of our own making? There absolutely are consequences for our actions and specifically for our sin (Heb 12:6), but God doesn't punish us nor is his mind about us changed based on our actions. His affection for us isn't based on us; it's based on him—on his mercy and grace toward sinners (Rom 5:8; 8:31-39; Eph 1:3-10; 2:4-5; 2 Tim 2:13).

A SUPERSTITIOUS FAITH

Some of us may not think that our actions earn God's favor or shield us from his punishment. Rather we have what I call a superstitious faith. We ask, "What will God do next?" and then reply, "It'll be just my luck for something terrible to happen."

Recently I was speaking with my husband about something, and I made this flippant comment. I can't remember exactly what I was referring to, but I will never forget his response: "Trillia, that's superstitious and sounds like you aren't trusting God." He had seen through my flippant comment and realized it wasn't flippant at all; it was a reflection of my heart.

His response stopped me in my tracks. I suddenly realized I'd been relating to life and God with superstition instead of faith throughout the past month. You see, we'd had a peaceful, joy-filled, easy month. We hadn't had any trials—at least none that stand out. It had been a slow month; I hadn't been traveling, the kids' activities were all but halted, and besides swimming our way through year-end paperwork, it had been easygoing.

And yet I was afraid. I feared the bottom would drop out and we'd find ourselves enduring a great trial. I'd been waiting for something horrible to happen that might ruin our happy month. And because I was holding the good things at arm's length, it was difficult to enjoy and thank God for the sweet rest of that season. I'd find myself thinking that my "lucky streak" would run out, and I'd get hit with something bad. I'd endured many trials in the past, and though I knew they were good and refining, I found myself anxious about what might be coming next.

As I thought about this struggle and tension, it reminded me of my third pregnancy. I had two miscarriages prior to that pregnancy, and I was terribly frightened that I'd lose the third child. It was difficult for me even to celebrate the pregnancy. At every appointment, I was sure I'd hear the dreaded words, "We don't hear a heartbeat." During those months, I had to learn to trust God and rest in him. I needed faith to believe that my pregnancy was a gift and that I could indeed enjoy it and thank him for it, even with a guarded heart.

This recent season of life felt similar, except there wasn't any tangible reason to fear. I'd simply looked to the future and even at God's way with a lack of trust—and even suspicion. So I'm learning all over again what it means to fight for faith, even in the midst of the joys of this life.

As I learn to trust him and fight for faith, God continues to remind me that he is indeed sovereign, but he is also oh so good. If God is only sovereign and not also good, there's reason to fear. But God is good and sovereign, and he has promised to do good (Ps 119:68). But his goodness doesn't equal a lack of trials. When I look to the unknown, I need not fear because I am in the hands of a good God—*not* because there are no troubles ahead. He is my Father, and I can rest and trust him. He is who he is, regardless of whether or not I believe it. But today I'm asking God to help me believe.

As the preacher of Ecclesiastes wrote, there is a time for everything (Eccles 3:1-8). For me, right now is a time for rejoicing.

My prayer for you and for me is that we learn to rejoice and dance and play and enjoy all that God is doing. And when the time comes for mourning, my prayer is that God will supply the grace needed in that season. But if that time is not now, let's put off fear and worry, and let's plead for faith to trust our good Father.

There is a constant battle in our race to remember to look to Jesus and trust our Father. We often find any reason to look away and try to make sense of life apart from him—even when times are good. But we need to fight against the ideas found in the prosperity gospel and the unfortunate reasons for superstitious faith. Why? Because life—the real Christian life—can be hard and wrought with pain and sorrow.

So, what do we do when suffering does come?

WHEN SUFFERING COMES

She was an active girl, riding horses, hiking, playing tennis, and swimming. On a summer day in 1967, all of that changed. In a matter of seconds, this young lady's life was changed forever. Miscalculating the depth of the Chesapeake Bay, Joni Eareckson Tada dove into the shallow water and hit her head, resulting in a catastrophic injury to her spine. She wouldn't walk again.

Joni was diagnosed as a quadriplegic, paralyzed from the shoulders down. In her autobiography, *Joni*, she shares the intimate details of the weeks, months, and years that would pass.[1] She tells of the days in the ICU, listening to new friends die in the bed beside her, visitors coming and going, and her attempt to reconcile God and the life she now would have.

Joni went on to marry, star in a movie about her story, start an organization for those with disabilities, and serve thousands upon thousands with her story and with her razor-sharp focus on God. She has endured great suffering and knows what it means to race through pain. She doesn't pretend that her sorrows aren't many and her pain isn't great. Instead she has spent her life focused on Jesus. She has endured well.

You and I may never have to endure the kind of suffering Joni has. But we have been promised that we will encounter trials and suffering. Jesus' life wasn't devoid of trials and suffering either, and it stands to reason that as we model our lives more and more after his, we too will endure trials as he did. God uses trials and suffering to transform us in this race that we're running. Qualities that will serve us well—our character, resolve, etc.—are shaped most significantly during such times.

The apostle Paul was a man who endured. He was persecuted, imprisoned, beaten—even to near death (2 Cor 11:21-23). If his troubles from those who persecuted him weren't enough, Paul also dealt with the elements as he traveled, warded off robbers, suffered from thirst and hunger, and faced accusations from people he served; even land and sea were dangers for him (2 Cor 11:24-29). But Paul didn't ask for any of these things to be taken away—perhaps because he had learned to be content (Phil 4:11-13). Or maybe it was because he had a consistent pain that was far worse. We'll never know why on this earth, but we do know Paul had a pain, a thorn in his side that he asked the Lord to get rid of (2 Cor 12:7-8).

No one knows what Paul's thorn was. There are many theories, but they are only theories. What we do know is that

Paul's thorn came from a messenger of Satan, similar to Job's experience (2 Cor 12:7; Job 1:1-12). We know it caused suffering, because he asked the Lord to remove it three times (2 Cor 12:8). And we know that Paul believed the purpose of his thorn was to keep him from being conceited. So, what can we learn from his thorn as it relates to enduring?

Enduring pain doesn't require that you ignore it or that you simply accept your fate. Paul asked the Lord to take his away. I used to think I had to be strong during trials. After my first of what would be four miscarriages, I mourned, but I thought I could just take a few deep breaths and move along. I wanted to be strong. For what reason, I still don't quite know. Perhaps my desire for strength was a sort of self-protection: *If I'm not vulnerable and weak, then I'll be okay.*

I'm glad God doesn't tell us to pull ourselves up by our bootstraps. He is near and loves the brokenhearted, the needy, and the weak. And as we read the psalms, we are invited to weep and mourn, to lament pain.

Why do you hide your face?
   Why do you forget our affliction and oppression?
For our soul is bowed down to the dust;
   our belly clings to the ground.
Rise up; come to our help!
   Redeem us for the sake of your steadfast love!
   (Ps 44:24-26)

We can ask the Lord hard questions: Where are you, Lord? How long, my God? Asking him for his presence and trying to gain understanding about a situation is not cursing him. As author and editor Al Hsu wrote, "Lament . . . focuses our grief in the proper direction—it turns us toward God."[2] As we lament, we can ask him to take the pain and suffering away. As far as we know, Paul died with that thorn in his side. The Lord didn't take it away. But his pain wasn't in vain; it had a great and good purpose.

When Paul asked that the pain be removed, God's response was "My grace is sufficient for you, for my power is made perfect in weakness" (2 Cor 12:9). Grace is poured out for the suffering. Grace is enough to sustain us. It isn't our strength that keeps us going; it's God's grace. For Paul, the danger could have been pride. Had he been completely strong and pain-free, he may have boasted about his good works and knowledge (2 Cor 12:7). But because he was weak, he knew it was only the Lord who was sustaining him; thus his boast was in the Lord.

I had it wrong after my first miscarriage. I thought it was up to me. I thought I needed to be strong. It wasn't until my second miscarriage that I understood that I had no strength to endure apart from the mercy and grace of our Lord. There wasn't anything I could do. I had many questions. But more than that, I had deep sorrow, and I mourned for several months. God's grace sustained me through the pain. And then I got pregnant again, and God sustained me through the fear and anxiety during that pregnancy—up until the very minute when my child was born.

God's grace is sufficient. Pain is hard, and he knows it. Enduring suffering is at times akin to torture, and he doesn't ask us to deny that. Sometimes we want to give up. He doesn't expect us to grin and bear it, and he doesn't leave us alone. "His grace is sufficient" means he is with you. He will sustain you with his righteous right hand.

FAITH IN THE FACE OF TROUBLES

Facing troubles takes *faith*.

Wait, didn't I just say the prosperity gospel is a distorted faith-based belief that God will give us what we want? Yes, I did. But just because we want to avoid the prosperity gospel, which attempts to use faith to achieve certainty in our health and wealth, doesn't mean we throw out faith altogether. The end of the prosperity gospel isn't the end we're aiming at. It takes faith to believe so that we may endure. Faith is precious and pleasing to God.

Faith is often associated with salvation: "By grace you have been saved through faith" (Eph 2:8). It also makes sense; everything about Christianity takes faith to believe. A man who was with God came to earth in the form of a baby, was perfect, died on a cross, bore the wrath of God, died, and rose. It takes faith to believe that.

C. S. Lewis put it this way:

> I am trying here to prevent anyone saying the really foolish thing that people often say about Him: I'm ready to accept Jesus as a great moral teacher, but I don't accept his claim to be God. That is the one thing we must not say. A man who was merely a man and said the sort of things Jesus said would not be a great moral teacher. He would either be a lunatic—on the level with the man who says he is a poached egg—or else he would be the Devil of Hell. You

must make your choice. Either this man was, and is, the Son of God, or else a madman or something worse. You can shut him up for a fool, you can spit at him and kill him as a demon or you can fall at his feet and call him Lord and God, but let us not come with any patronizing nonsense about his being a great human teacher. He has not left that open to us. He did not intend to. . . . Now it seems to me obvious that He was neither a lunatic nor a fiend: and consequently, however strange or terrifying or unlikely it may seem, I have to accept the view that He was and is God.[3]

It takes faith to believe God is who he says he is. It takes faith to believe the claims of Christianity. It either is what it is or it is all a lie. Our belief is a gift from God (Eph 2:8).

The same applies to enduring pain. "Now faith is the assurance of things hoped for, the conviction of things not seen" (Heb 11:1). In order for Paul to keep going through his pain, he had to believe that there was a purpose in it and that the purpose was greater than him. He had to believe that God would do as he said, that God would sustain him. To keep going through pain, we too must have faith.

I will never forget a bike ride I had with a good girlfriend. We were in Utah for a visit and decided to hit the road. Meg was skilled on the bike and was able to bike long distances without much food. We started before eating lunch, and two hours in without any food on us, only water, we were still riding. I was doing great until about mile twenty. As if I had cycled right into a wall, my legs didn't want to move, my stomach began to ache, and I thought I might faint. I was miserable, hungry, and tired.

Did I mention that we were riding in high altitude? Yes, I was also out of oxygen.

I was a mess. I didn't know how to get back to water, food, and rest except to follow her home. And I did. "We're getting closer," she said. "Almost there, Trill." I was blind. I was in pain. Slowly, painfully, I cycled behind her to relief. The ride had been a memorable mess.

It took a lot of trust and a lot of faith for me to believe Meg. I had to believe that she had my absolute best interest in mind and would get me there before I fainted. She did. I wanted to cry a few times, and at times we laughed hysterically. And we made it. I followed, trusted, and kept moving.

The faith it took to get through this experience doesn't compare to the faith I needed when I was pregnant. It doesn't compare to the sort of faith it takes when someone receives a terrible diagnosis. But it illustrates how, as we are enduring in this life, as we are going through pain, we do so blindly. You and I don't know the end; only God does. All we have is faith. We cling to faith. We pray by faith. We trust by faith. It's all about faith. And it's all a gift of his grace.

God gives us the faith to believe that which is unseen. We find our heart's rest in knowing that the God that is unseen is with us. God gives us faith to believe that he is who he says he is in his Word. He gives us faith to believe that all his promises are indeed ours. He gives us faith to believe that Jesus is interceding for us. And when we don't believe, when our faith seems frail, we rest in his promise to never leave us nor forsake us. As theologian J. I. Packer once said, "Your faith will not fail while

God sustains it; you are not strong enough to fall away while God is resolved to hold you."[4]

In the next few chapters, we'll look at some real-life circumstances that make enduring difficult. I've intentionally divided our specific struggles into three areas. The first is mind pain. These are the things that happen in us. They may be the result of circumstances, or they may simply be unseen struggles such as cynicism, jadedness, weariness, burnout, and complacency. The second is body pain, things that happen to us, such as cancer, car wrecks, or some other circumstances. Finally we'll look at our current culture and connected world. We are in a time right now when there is a great need to endure—and obstacles to it—at every turn. Through all of these real circumstances, we learn to walk in faith and not by sight, knowing that God is continually and always with us.

GOD'S PRESENCE TO ENDURE

Writer and author Randy Alcorn reflected on 1 Peter 4 as he retold the story of one of the greatest trials of his life and all that the Lord had brought him through. He concluded, "'Dear friends, don't be surprised when a fiery trial comes, as though something strange were happening to you.' We have never bought into prosperity theology. During my trials I've had an acute awareness of God's presence."

Randy is no stranger to tragedy. As he is acutely aware of God's presence, he's also acutely aware that godliness, faith, and obedience do not guarantee a life of ease.

At thirty-one, the seemingly healthy Randy was diagnosed with type 1 diabetes. His diagnosis came the same month his

first book was released. This was one of the first major altera-
tions of his life. Randy had grown up independent and had
always been strong and healthy. But his body had critical needs
simply to survive. "It was the Lord's way of both humbling me
and make me dependent on him," he said.

Five years later, in 1990, he faced another test when he was
arrested for blocking the doors of abortion clinics. One of the
clinics sued him and lost but won a settlement. But Randy's
conscience wouldn't allow him to pay; he didn't want to write
a check to an abortion provider. At some time before that, all
of his assets had been put in the name of Nanci, his wife, and
100 percent of his royalties for book sales had been allocated
to a ministry. By law, he was broke.

At the time of the incident, Randy was the pastor of a large
church. He had to resign to protect the church from financial
ruin, fearing that the courts would come after the church for
payment. He was already living on a small portion of his salary,
and he had just paid off his home. Another court case involving
another abortion clinic followed. They were awarded the largest
judgment ever against a group of peaceful protestors:
$8.2 million. Randy needed to make minimum wage or less to
keep from having his wages garnished.

Amazingly he exclaimed, "The greatest gifts the Lord has
given me are both trials." Since then the judgment ended, and
he's now able to earn higher wages. But, he said, "It was actually easier when we made minimum wage." Recently he and
Nanci had to spend $25,000 on a home repair. They continue
to have his royalties go to his ministry.

During these years, Randy has battled depression but says he has never once doubted the goodness of God. He quickly proclaimed, "The Lord sustained me."

Now he and Nanci are facing yet another battle. She has been diagnosed with cancer. "We have talked a lot about our mortality," Randy said. "Not in a morbid way. We ask about wanting to finish well. We will not reach our peaks until the resurrection. No more pain. Front-loading the eternal realities today brings us peace and joy for today."

About a bucket list, he said, "Do you think the only time to climb a mountain will be in this world?"[5]

Only the real God can sustain us in our trials—not cheap substitutes. He will surely do it.

ENDURING AND THE MIND

Have you ever had someone share something with you but start out with several caveats? Or maybe someone was hoping to work with you on something but first explained all the reasons you should work with someone else. Well, that's what I'm about to do here. I want to explain what I'm *not* doing in this chapter and where I'm *not* qualified before diving into all the ways we struggle through pain.

I'm not writing this as a psychologist, therapist, or certified Christian counselor. I'm writing as a layperson who has studied God's Word and who has also experienced the topics I'm writing on either firsthand or through friendships with others. As you read this chapter, you may discover that your best next step is to see a counselor who can help you most effectively. Although my hope and prayer is that this chapter is useful to you as we run this race, I'm also aware that some struggles need the attention of a trained professional.

With that said, let's explore the first area that needs our attention: the mind. Our minds are utterly important to our walk of faith.

THE IMPORTANCE OF THE MIND

Endurance athletes have been known to say that finishing a race is as much about their minds as about their skill—if not more. Of course, skill matters, but if your mind isn't ready to get to mile thirteen in a marathon and continue running thirteen more miles, the chances of you finishing are slim. The longest I've ever run is six miles, and right now running even one mile is pure agony. My body can keep going, but my mind says, "Stop!"

Endurance athlete Dean Karnazes completed fifty marathons in fifty states in fifty consecutive days. He wanted to test his physical limits, but that's not all.

> Once I did a marathon, I thought, "Huh, I think I can go further than this." I wanted to explore not only my physical limits but my mental confines. As research shows, part of an athlete's training includes methods for dealing with pain. Some distract themselves by reciting poems or counting strokes. These athletes are actively engaging their minds to run the race set before them. Although to us their work looks effortless, they are working both physically and mentally to endure to the end.[1]

The mind is incredible and powerful. It is the powerhouse of all our systems. The US National Library of Medicine says this about the brain: "The brain works like a big computer. It processes information that it receives from the senses and body, and sends messages back to the body. But the brain can do much more than a machine can: humans think and experience emotions with their brain, and it is the root of human intelligence."[2]

The brain allows you and me to know when something is hot to the touch, signals to our senses that we should fight or flee, and allows us to look at these words right now and interpret them. As we do simple things like begin to take one step forward, our mind has already told our muscles to move. It's miraculous what God has created and how it functions.

That's one of many reasons it's so devastating when a brain is injured. The brain controls just about everything in us: our responses, our reactions, our movement, our words, and even our affections. God knows this. God designed it to be so. And at one time our minds were perfect.

But injury isn't the only threat to our brains. The sin in Genesis 3 did damage to all things, including our minds.

As Romans 1:28 explains, in our sin nature—before we were transformed by the gospel—we had a debased mind. This means our minds, before we become Christians, don't have the ability to make us love God; our thoughts are unable to please God. And then we have the impossible command to love God not just with our hearts, but with all of who we are, including our minds (Mt 22:37).

Here's the good news: the problem of our minds and our inability to please God has been solved through the blood of Jesus. When he transforms us, he transforms us entirely. That doesn't mean we are healed of injury to the brain, and it doesn't mean we have no need to use our mind. It does mean that our deepest and greatest need to be washed and made clean has been satisfied. Yet as you and I know, the struggle to control the mind remains, and the Scriptures have a lot to say about it.

THE SILENT BATTLE AGAINST CYNICISM

I usually listen to music as I get ready for the day, but lately, in an effort to be informed about the world and keep up with current events, I've been listening to National Public Radio. I use the Alexa app, that personified application device that plays music and will even talk to you. Recently, after doing my normal routine, I went to shut off Alexa. But I discovered that it wasn't on.

I was certain I had been listening to something. Then I realized that my thoughts were so loud, I'd forgotten to ask Alexa to play something. My mind was going a mile a minute with thoughts about the day, my schedule, a conflict that needed resolution, and so on. I can't recall all that was on my mind, but my thoughts were loud. *That* I remember clearly.

Our mind battles are typically silent—that is, silent to others. But they're loud in our heads. I've found these struggles hard to articulate. It's easy to say, "I am anxious about . . . ," but to fully grasp the weight of the anxiety, we need to be in our heads. And because mind battles are silent, it's easy to think we're alone. But we aren't alone in this fight.

Plenty has been written about anxiety, depression, worry, and the like. And we can never tire of working through those battles. Some of those struggles have to do with chemical imbalances or hormonal issues. Thankfully the church is beginning to pay greater attention to that.

One struggle I haven't seen addressed much in Christian ministry—but that can deeply affect the way we view God and neighbor—is *cynicism*. By definition, cynicism is "an inclination to believe that people are motivated purely by self-interest."[3] Its sister's name is *skepticism*. The cynic doesn't trust or believe others. Over time people affected by cynicism may become jaded or apathetic. They've been disappointed or seen something too much, so they give up. Both cynicism and skepticism can eventually lead to weariness, especially with the Christian walk or Christianity.

I've seen churches divide, friends walk away from one another, and people not bearing with one another because cynicism crept in and took over. When we see a leader fall, for example, it can be difficult to bear another controversy yet again in the church. We may throw in the towel and give up.

I had known Sarah and loved her dearly for several years. She was someone I looked up to, someone who loved God. I wanted to imitate her faith. Her life was rather simple—one might say easy. But then her faith began to crumble, though her husband remained faithful and her children were stable and incredibly obedient. Nothing had happened to her—no sickness, no financial problems. So what happened? A leader we trusted and followed had fallen into sin, and everything she knew began to crumble.

Sarah's response was to run away from it all. But she didn't only leave the church; she left the faith. She had become cynical, and she could no longer trust anyone. She was jaded—no longer willing to bear the burdens of others. Sarah spent nights reading articles about this fallen leader and seethed over the destruction he left behind. She couldn't focus, and she struggled to get it off her mind. Eventually everyone seemed to be liars and cheats to her. Who could she trust?

I empathize with Sarah. It's terrible when everything you thought was true comes undone. Lies are revealed. People are betrayed. It's beyond difficult. Leaving a church is absolutely acceptable and at times necessary. What I've wrestled with, however, was how jadedness and cynicism can lead us to renounce our faith in God. If this person could do this to that person, then how could God be good and trustworthy? These situations and how we respond to them are complicated, but seeing how fallen people wreck lives has helped me evaluate where I place my affections. Where we set our hearts and minds truly matters. Where we place our affections affects our view of all things.

A cynic struggles to see the beauty and possibilities in others or in circumstances. Essayist Marilynne Robinson put it clearly: "When a good man or woman stumbles, we say, 'I knew it all along,' and when a bad one has a gracious moment, we sneer at the hypocrisy. It is as if there is nothing to mourn or to admire, only a hidden narrative now and then apparent through the false, surface narrative. And the hidden narrative, because it is ugly and sinister, is therefore true."[4]

No matter what good comes, it is clouded by the memories of disappointments. To be sure, it may be true that someone wronged you, but it isn't true that everyone is after you. It may be true that your pastor betrayed the trust of his family and congregation, but it isn't true that every pastor will. And it may be true that people can be untrustworthy, but it isn't true that God is.

A fight against cynicism is a fight to see beauty and grace. One way to fight this temptation is to renew our minds—to replace thoughts that have entered with true thoughts. Look for beauty. Look for good. See the lovely things in God's creation. They are there if we'd only look. Jesus has given you and me a way of escape from our cynicism; we can choose to see the good in others and in circumstances (1 Cor 10:13).

So, what does fighting cynicism look like practically? Paul began the last chapter of Philippians by expressing his sincere and deep love for the church in Philippi. After that one line, he took a swift turn to discuss two members of the church, Euodia and Syntyche (Phil 4:2). There had been a conflict between the two women. We don't know the details, but it must have been significant for it to make its way not only into Paul's letter to the church but also into the Word of God. This is a good indication that this seemingly insignificant event is important, so we ought to pay attention.

We don't know specifics about the situation, but we do know that Paul entreated Euodia and Syntyche to "agree in the Lord" (Phil 4:2). He wanted them to be of the same mind, same love, and in full accord with one another, as was his desire for the entire church (Phil 2:2). These two needed a third-party intervention to help them reconcile. This reveals the importance of community in the life of believers. We can't work out our struggles on our own; we need the help of fellow believers to mediate, encourage, exhort, and support us. Focusing on our minds isn't enough; placing ourselves in the context of communities keeps us going.

Perhaps Paul longed to see the two women united because of their partnership in gospel ministry (Phil 4:3). But I find especially interesting his instruction after this introductory paragraph urging the women to reconcile. Paul then exhorted the church to rejoice, be reasonable, resist being anxious, and pray and give thanks (Phil 4:4-6). His final instruction involved their thinking as he told them to think thoughts that are true, honorable, just, pure, lovely, commendable, excellent, and praiseworthy (Phil 4:8).

Why would Paul instruct two sisters in their thinking after addressing a conflict between them? Let's think about our own conflicts. What happens to your mind when you have a misunderstanding with someone? I know I can be tempted to do the opposite of what Paul is encouraging here. It takes great effort to be reasonable and even greater to think true thoughts. What's lovely and commendable? Acts of self-control, love, and bearing with others do not happen apart from the work of the Holy Spirit.

Paul's instructions to the Philippians are for us too. We have to work to fill our minds with true, pure, and honorable thoughts. As we engage others and the world around us, we remind ourselves, "The Lord is at hand." God isn't wringing his hands, and he has not left us. Because we know that God is working and active in all situations, we can submit our anxious thoughts to him. Fixing our minds on him can bring us peace that "surpasses all understanding" and guards our hearts and minds in Christ Jesus (Phil 4:7).

What might our fight against cynicism look like using the scenario above (a fallen pastor) and applying Philippians 4? Here are three possibilities:

- ■ *Affirm whatever is true.* Not all leaders are committing adultery or living secret lives.
- ■ *Affirm whatever is honorable.* If the church or its leaders handled the situation in a proper manner, thank God.

■ *Affirm whatever is just.* Vengeance is the Lord's, and every person walking this earth will give an account. I don't need to hold on to bitterness as a way to punish that person or organization.

And so on.

We can apply this exercise to many things to help guard our minds and to turn them toward true thoughts, which will increase our affection for the Lord and guard our walk. If we want to endure, we must fight the temptation to be cynical. Cynicism doesn't seem dangerous—until it is. You and I can ask the Lord to help us set our minds on things above (Col 3:2). Part of guarding our minds and loving God with our minds is increasing our knowledge of Jesus and pondering the great things of God. Think on him when you find yourself wondering if there's anything good and worthy. *He* is.

PUSHING AWAY COMPLACENCY

Another area not often addressed as a threat to our faith is *complacency*. Some people chalk complacency up to our actions, but it starts with our minds. By definition, complacency is "a feeling of smug or uncritical satisfaction with oneself or one's achievements."[5] How we think about ourselves and how we think about our Lord greatly affects our actions. If you think, for example, that you've "arrived," that you've achieved intellectual and spiritual perfection, you aren't likely to study God's Word. Or maybe you do, but your purpose is to learn about God and to pray for the Word to transform you so you can puff yourself up.

Why is this a threat? Because the proud do not need God. It's hard to be vulnerable and dependent on God if you're self-assured and self-reliant. For example, Isaiah warned the women of Jerusalem against complacency. They had become comfortable and self-indulgent; they were haughty and being called to repentance (Is 3:16-17; 32:9-20).

Most who are complacent may not even realize it. The kind of complacency I'm referring to rarely looks like pride. It's not about throwing around Bible verses or self-righteously judging others. It could manifest itself as "going through the motions"— doing all the outward churchy things we know we're "supposed" to do while our affections are far from the Lord.

The church in Sardis suffered from complacency and didn't know. John's words help us see the error in the church through the words of Jesus: "I know your works. You have the reputation of being alive, but you are dead. Wake up, and strengthen what remains and is about to die, for I have not found your works complete in the sight of my God" (Rev 3:1-2). They were thought to be alive and thriving and yet were not. Jesus told the church to remember the message of grace they received, to keep it and repent (Rev 3:3). They were going through the motions and had forgotten the message and the messenger. They were culturally good yet spiritually dead.

I pray against this and am watchful of it as I raise my children. I didn't grow up in a Christian home, so when I became a Christian as an adult, it was all new and fresh and exciting to me. But my children are growing up in a Christian home, so we need to guard against complacency. They're familiar with the Bible, with church, and with the various things associated with the Christian faith. I pray that they'll be smitten with God, over the hill in love with Jesus. But I know it will be a fight. Perhaps you relate.

A friend shared once that she was simply bored with the Christian life. She felt it was dry. She was going to church, but even that started to feel like a chore. In many ways, without the feelings of cynicism, she was a bit jaded. She wondered, *What's the point of it all?* There were two key reasons for her complacency: (1) she was extremely busy, so the outward expressions of her faith were just one more thing on her to-do list, and (2) she didn't think she had anything new to learn.

Perhaps cynicism is fed by a false ideal of how life should be lived. The American dream sells us a vision a life filled with adventure, fun, and excitement. We live by empty slogans like "Work hard to play hard" and "Take life by the horns." But life often looks like cleaning toilets and paying bills. And in our Bible study times with the Lord, we aren't likely to be taken up to the third heaven. They are more likely times of exploring and reading and learning things we've seen before. The Bible is not boring—please don't get me wrong—but our daily reading of it is often simple and ordinary.

The Christian life is mundane. We repeat the same things day after day. But it's a life of abundance—not because we get adventure or fun, but because we get Christ. As Thomas Chalmers spoke in a sermon about worldliness, "The heart is not so constituted; and the only way to dispossess it of an old affection, is by the expulsive power of a new one."[6]

Over the past few years, as technology has crept more and more into my life, my phone has become a strange source of comfort, curiosity, and misplaced affection. I have access to old friends, new friends, acquaintances, news, unfortunate gossip, and much more at the click of a button. At one point I realized that my affection for my phone had replaced my desire for my morning reading time in God's Word. Instead of reading I'd check my phone, and the next thing I knew it was time to start my day.

The phone was an ordinary thing, but it had invaded the most precious time I had with the Lord. I had to replace that affection for a new (or shall I say renewed) affection for the Lord. That meant practicing self-control in the morning and waiting to check my phone. As I've disposed of this old affection, the Lord has stirred my heart once again for time in the morning with him. God has given me a new affection.

My phone example may seem simple and not much of a threat to our race. Yet sometimes it's the simple, mundane, and ordinary things in life, such as the distraction of our phones, that keep us from what used to be our first love. To fight complacency we need to renew our affection for the Lord. Our words may not be eloquent, but we can simply ask: Lord, make you my first love. Give me a desire for you, knowing that I already have your affection.

THE UPWARD CALL

Both the cynic and the complacent—and all of us—could be helped by Paul's example and his warnings in Philippians 3. He warned the Philippians to watch out for those who practiced outwardly obeying the law but not worshiping God. These people had put their confidence in the flesh (Phil 3:2-3). Paul then listed all the reasons the world and the society at that time would have confidence in his flesh: he was the cream of the crop of that time, religious, a persecutor, of the right pedigree (Phil 3:4-6). But none of this mattered. None of his worldly accolades mattered compared to knowing Jesus. He counted it all as rubbish (Phil 3:8). Upon Paul's conversion to Christianity, he lost all his status in society. He lost it *all*. All the prestige—all of it—gone.

His loss was all a gain. He wanted to be found in Jesus. He knew that his righteousness was not based on his good works but rather on the righteousness from God. Paul wanted to finish the race set before him. He wanted to know the power of Jesus' resurrection and become like his Savior—by any means of suffering necessary (Phil 3:11).

I long to know Christ and only Christ as Paul did. There seemed to be a deep crying out in his soul to be with Jesus. It would have been easy for Paul to become puffed up. He may not have been much in society after his conversion, but he was a leader in the first-century church. He was not as we see in verse twelve: "Not that I have already obtained this or am already perfect, but I press on to make it my own, because Christ Jesus has made me his own." Paul was not perfect. He was running toward something. He was motivated in all his loss to press on toward something, toward someone. "I press on toward the goal for the prize of the upward call of God in Christ Jesus" (Phil 3: 14).

There's a prize awaiting all of us. Paul ran his race looking toward that prize. We'll explore the prize more fully in chapter twelve, but Paul explained that the mature know they need to grow in Christ and continue to learn and repent (Phil 3:15). We haven't arrived, we aren't perfect, and we'll never be until that day we see Jesus face to face and obtain the prize. Paul was pressing toward that goal: resurrected, glorified bodies fully knowing and worshiping our Savior for eternity.

Let this vision and knowledge of our Lord Jesus Christ motivate you to fight and press on toward this upward call. We are in a race, and the finish line is closer than we could imagine. But we've got to get there.

Paul ended this chapter with a sober warning that the worldly among them wouldn't end the race well: "Their end is destruction, their god is their belly, and they glory in their shame, with minds set on earthly things" (Phil 3:19). They had a problem, and their problem involved their minds. They needed a new affection.

For true believers, our citizenship is in heaven (Phil 3:20). To set our minds on anything else will lead to despair and discouragement—and away from our Savior. Where we set our minds matters. Think on the things above. Think of what you'll be there. It isn't selfish to look forward to the day we'll no longer have these lowly, broken bodies. We will have glorious bodies and glorious minds, no longer divided and torn. Our minds will be clear, with no more fog and confusion.

Can you imagine what it will be like to have complete clarity? To no longer despair? To never be disappointed or to disappoint others? Despondency—gone. Discouragement—gone. Cynicism and complacency—forever gone. This is what we have to look forward to. But we don't have to wait until that day to meditate on our reality. We can think about it now. I long to have mature thinking, which means a mind set on the things above. Setting our minds on Jesus and the prize that we're running toward allows for greater endurance in this race.

RENEWING OUR MINDS

Paul urged the Christians in Rome not to be conformed to this world, but be transformed by the renewal of their minds (Rom 12:1-2). R. C. Sproul commented on this, saying, "We see that Christianity is a faith of both mind and heart. God does not call us to surrender our rational faculties when we trust in His Son; rather, it is only in serving Him that we use our minds as He created them to be used."[7]

Our minds were meant to worship God; that's what he always intended for us. Although we know that what's wrong will one day be made right, we don't want to wait until that day to begin renewing our minds.

Today you and I can begin this renewal, whether for the first time or for the hundredth, by filling our minds with the promises of God. None of what I've written above and what I'll write for the rest of this book will matter if we aren't meditating on the Word day and night (Ps 1:2). You will need to scream to your heart and mind that pursuing Jesus with all you have is not legalism; in many ways, it's survival. Let's engage our minds in the race of endurance.

My friend was in town, visiting for a conference. Within a moment, every plan for her day, for her future, for her life was in question. One split-second decision regarding the mundane everyday act of stepping off a curb into a crosswalk left her hanging in the balance between life and death. She had been hit by a bus.

Unexpected circumstances affect and plague us all the time. You've heard the stories and perhaps experienced them yourself. You're seemingly fine one day, healthy with no signs that anything could be wrong, and the next day after a scan or routine checkup, you're diagnosed with a disease that will control the next few years of your life or potentially lead you straight to your Savior. Everything is changed in an instant.

I've experienced this devastating reality with family and friends. It's hard to make sense of it all. For some, the physical pain is difficult but manageable with medicine. Again, it's the mind that's in the fight.

"Where are you, Lord?"

"Why did you allow this to happen to me?"

"Will I recover?"

"Will I be the same?"

These are some of the thoughts that may plague you even today.

The mind helps us process not only what's going on in us but also the things that happen to us. How we respond to various trials depends on our thoughts. I recently had a teaching opportunity for my son in which I realized just how much our experiences can affect us for life.

With the earth tilted just enough to bring the warm air consistently into our area, our kids grabbed their bikes to ride outside until sunset. A recent rainstorm chased them inside, but it was no surprise that once the light again broke through the clouds, the kids were back out the door to their bikes. The only problem was that neither was adept at riding in wet conditions. So lo and behold, when my six-year-old son turned on his favorite curve, the wheel came out from under him, skidding on the gravel—and down he went.

When he came into the house, battered and bruised, humiliated and in pain, his father didn't say to him, "Suck it up, son. Get over it and stop your whining." No, he asked if he was okay. He comforted him. He bandaged his knee and set him on his way to play again.

Later I spoke with our son about the mechanics of riding in the wet—which were, basically, go slow. I told him how excited I would be to ride with him when it was dry outside. I wanted to encourage him to endure, to learn to keep going, and not to give up in the face of adversity. Sure, he had just bumped his knee, but it had taken him several years to get back on the bike the first time he wrecked.

After I finished my encouragement, he said to me, "I can't wait to ride with you!"

Whew.

Although his small bike incident was inconsequential, life regularly provides opportunities for us to reflect on the Lord's teaching—in this case, on suffering and endurance. It was like a modern-day parable that reminded me of Paul's words, guided by the Holy Spirit: "We rejoice in our sufferings, knowing that suffering produces endurance, and endurance produces character, and character produces hope, and hope does not put us to shame, because God's love has been poured into our hearts through the Holy Spirit who has been given to us" (Rom 5:3-5).

We might read these verses and think that the command is for us to be happy and excited about suffering. But the thought of rejoicing in suffering is preposterous to most. Others might think it's an ungracious, unrealistic approach to the real challenges of pain. We might even quote the Bible back at the Bible: "You mean mourn with those who mourn, right? But Paul didn't write, 'Rejoice in suffering because suffering produces glad and happy feelings.'" No, we rejoice in suffering because suffering produces character and namely the character of Christ. The funny thing is that this sort of character transformation does produce joy, but our rejoicing is always based in Christ and not in how we feel.

GOD'S GIFT OF ENDURANCE

Suffering produces the endurance required to keep going in the faith as we wait for the day we will no longer suffer. Enduring doesn't mean ignoring the pain or trouble. As I've learned to endure in suffering, I've discovered that to acknowledge the reality of the pain and to keep going in the strength that God provides. When God says that when we are weak, then we are strong, he means it. Endurance in suffering isn't about pulling ourselves up by our bootstraps; instead it's about falling into the arms of our Father to receive help in our times of need. Endurance in suffering helps us to persevere.

In times of trial, our confidence must be placed solely on our Lord. Our Lord, our true hope, will not put us to shame. After my son's bike accident, my husband could have said something to make him feel ignorant and weak. He could have shamed him for riding in the rain. Although it wasn't our son's fault that he fell, he did make the decision to ride the bike in conditions that weren't ideal.

Many times I've chastised my children for making unwise decisions. The chastisement that we are rightly due because of our sins has been covered. Jesus took the chastisement of us all (Is 53:5). And so as we suffer and endure trials, we know that we won't be put to shame. We can have hope because we know the end of the story. We know that one day all our pain and suffering will be wiped away. Our faith is in Jesus and his finished work.

So we rejoice because we trust that what God says in his Word is true. We rejoice because we know that suffering produces character, and in our hope, he will not put us to shame. We rejoice because we know that rejoicing isn't about our feelings or our abilities to perform. Instead it's about resting in Jesus and remembering the joy that awaits us. We fix our eyes on Jesus because he suffered on our behalf, and as our perfect model, he too was looking toward the joy set before him (Heb 12:2). Our joy may not come in the morning. It may take years before we're able to rejoice in our suffering. God is patient. And it's our aim to rejoice, though it may be a painful hallelujah over the course of many pleas for help.

> You keep him in perfect peace
>> whose mind is stayed on you,
>> because he trusts in you. (Is 26:3)

RUNNING WITH THE PAIN

My thirty-four-year-old friend Andrew recently told me what he would say to his sixteen-year-old self as he reflected on his painful memories of a horrific skiing accident that almost took his life: "This situation you are in is no doubt unspeakably difficult, but God has the ability to use circumstances like this to teach you things that you may not learn until sixteen to seventeen years down the road. You cannot plot and plan. I'm not downplaying the difficulty of your pain, but I have not seen God not use something to teach those involved."

Andrew would say that what happened to him at sixteen uniquely shaped the man he is today. He was extremely athletic in high school. Running was his passion, though he would take it further and say it was his identity. He believed that he would one day run in college and likely earn a scholarship. In prime running condition, he decided to take up a different sport for a day and went on a skiing trip with friends. He had never skied before, so it would be quite the adventure.

On April 18, 2001, while skiing down a medium-grade hill, Andrew lost control and hit a tree. "I hit a tree—going so fast. I put my arm up to protect my head so my midsection took the brunt of the hit," he recalled. Remarkably he didn't break a bone, but he did have internal bleeding and a lacerated liver. "I was alert and conscious for maybe five or ten minutes. After then I went into ischemia, where the blood supply decreases. I went into shock."

He remembered anguishing pain. He spent forty-four days in a hospital, twenty-seven days in critical care, had eight operations to repair his liver, and spent two weeks in an induced coma. He had to learn to walk again. "I went from running almost sub-five-minute miles to having legs like tree trunks." Although this affected his body, it also affected his mind as he suffered from post-traumatic stress syndrome throughout high school. "I was an emotional wreck," he explained. As difficult as it was to experience PTSD, he could have easily had a severe and irreparable brain injury because he went without oxygen to his brain for more than four minutes. "Running literally saved my life because of the oxygen in my blood," he said.

Andrew was used to dealing with a certain level of pain. He had learned to endure and persevere, and he had the tenacity to see things through. What he didn't know was that a split-second trip would end with him in a coma, looking at years of recovery and a lifetime of ailments. "Running—you have to deal with pain. It's not that endurance runners decrease their pain; they learn to deal with it and grapple with it." Interestingly Andrew shared that a disproportionate number of people in the sport have experienced trauma. "We endure because it's both painful and also beautiful. We subject our bodies to pain. There's a level of human performance where people feel joy in the slog of running."

This outlook, the support and care of his high school girlfriend now wife, Christian, and the support of his church and friends helped Andrew recover in a miraculous way and pick back up the sport he so loves. His accident left him with *diastasis recti* (a lack of abdominal muscles in his lower abdomen), neuropathy, and hammertoes. The first time he ran again, he remembered thinking if he could just run for thirty minutes, it would be like a marathon. He did it, and though he was tired and in pain, it was exhilarating.

In January 2014, Andrew was running from time to time. In December 2014, he had a life-changing surgery on his right foot to repair his hammertoe condition. The reconstruction surgery allowed him to resume running on a regular basis.

Since then, with the encouragement, prayer, and partnership with his good friend and running partner, Jimmy, Andrew has run half and full marathons. "Jimmy takes such joy in catapulting me into this, helping someone succeed," he shared. "Augustine talks about having rightly ordered loves. I've been able to identify a thing that I love and to commit wholeheartedly to it. If what we are loving is truly worth loving and good, it produces joy. I have found loves that are worth loving for their own purpose, because they testify to God's design for us both physically and intellectually."

Andrew says he has always had an abiding faith in God. "I've never felt God is not there. You don't have to convince people to participate in things that they love—the question then is, is that thing worth loving? People are going to endure when they find that which they love."

And we endure in the faith because we've found that which is worthy of our love.

ENDURING IN SOCIETY
AND THE WORLD

I always find it peculiar that the Lord chose to put me in this particular place and time in history. What if we were born in a different era? What would have been going on during that time? With all the various advances and kingdoms and people throughout time, there's been one recurring theme throughout the history of time: trouble in the world. There's been war and division and unrest and confusion since Genesis 3. So I'm not surprised that in today's culture we're experiencing much of the same (1 Pet 4:12). Yet we still need to learn how to endure it all because it affects the race set before us.

LIVING IN A VIRTUAL WORLD

When I first began to dabble in social media, some ten years ago, it seemed to be a rather carefree place to share ideas and encouragement. Maybe we were all figuring it out back then but like many good things, it came to an end. No, social media isn't slowing down or losing popularity. Social media hasn't come to an end. Rather the good that was so often shared has taken a drastic turn. Much of our virtual world is filled with vitriol, anger, slander, bearing false witness, and your occasional cat video. And this isn't the "world" as we might say—it's Christians who are tearing one another a part.

Social media has been affecting us in ways we won't truly understand for many years. And what concerns me isn't our attachment to social media, although there's plenty to be concerned with there. It isn't the potential to curate our own personality or show only the happy times. My concern is the rhetoric. The way we engage one another has done great damage to our Christian witness and to our souls.

Recently I was speaking with a woman who expressed a desire to know the Lord but an uncertainty about attending church. I was explaining that she would likely be able to find a good church, but before I finished my thought, she said with a hint of exasperation, "Well, I saw a pastor on social media say something that was vulgar and unkind, and I decided not to go there." She wasn't talking about the church I was going to suggest, but her taste of Christian engagement on the internet had been enough to keep her from trying out a church—maybe any church.

Of course pastors aren't the only ones with "Jesus is my everything" in their profile and "I hate everyone" on their timeline. There's something quick and easy about typing out thoughts with little to no regard for how the words will affect the watching world. I've done it. I've had to go back and delete things I typed out of anger or out of ignorance. Let's consider this warning in Proverbs: "When words are many, transgression is not lacking, but whoever restrains his lips is prudent" (Prov 10:19). This doesn't mean we sit around silently; it means we consider our words.

One way to fight the temptation to express hatred and sow discord through our words on social media is to be slow to speak (Jas 1:19) and abounding in love. There are times when being silent and listening is the best witness you or I can have on social media. We don't have to jump into every controversy. We are free to ask hard questions before sharing our opinion. We are free to "walk in a manner worthy of the Lord" (Col 1:10). And when we do speak, we can do it by the power and grace of God, with both truth and love (Eph 4:15).

It's hard to endure when you're constantly upset with the church because of what you see or engage in via the internet. I'm an advocate for gaining knowledge, being informed, and keeping up with what's going on in the world. (A friend once said, "Ignorance is not bliss; it's just ignorance.") But with all the information we consume throughout each day, I've wondered if it's possible to sit and watch a sunset without worrying or thinking? Are we able to sit and enjoy our surroundings? Do we ever shut off our minds? The answer is likely *sometimes*, but more than likely *hardly*. World events aren't the only things that keep our minds spinning; we also have daily mundane tasks, unfinished projects, broken relationships, worries about finances—the list goes on and on because the cares of this world are many.

MANY OPINIONS, MANY BURDENS

The internet has enabled us to reveal where we stand on social issues, which has had a major effect on the church. I've experienced my fair share of hardships in this world, specifically regarding race relations. I'm an African American female living in the South, which has been a great joy and also at times painful.[1] It's easy for many to assume that because we are sixty years out from the civil rights movement and because laws have changed, we have arrived. I have been told that if I stop talking, writing, and speaking about race, the troubles will go away.

Race is one of the most charged topics. Most people have an opinion, and those opinions run deep. But for me, it's more than a topic. Race, racial reconciliation, racial harmony—you name it—is about people made in the image of God. And it's not a topic I can just ignore. As a black female in predominantly white spaces, I face the reality of my ethnicity every single day. This isn't a bad thing; it's simply reality. I often walk into a room and find there's no one else there who looks like me.

"We are past the civil rights movement, and surely we are all past the race issue," I've heard. My short answer to that is no, we aren't past these issues. People are quite unaware of the struggles of various members of our society. Just recently I shared a picture of my husband (who is white) and me as we lamented and celebrated the fifty-year anniversary of the legalization of interracial marriage. Many of my friends didn't know that something so precious as interracial marriage was illegal in our country at one point in time (and as recently as fifty years ago). I imagine that those who became aware gained a deeper understanding of the pain that many African Americans continue to feel in this country. Fifty years wasn't that long ago.

Why do I share this here and now in a book about enduring in the faith? My test, so to speak, has been enduring in both the evangelical church and our society, which have shown their cards. Social media, video recordings, and the like have exposed our culture for what it is. I had experienced blatant racism in my early years, but it was in the South, where politeness reigns even if fake. It wasn't typically hostile. (However, once a friend and I were walking down the street when a man threw a brick and yelled an explicit racial term at us.) But over the past few years, people from white supremacist organizations have harassed me on social media and websites, calling me names. We are in a tumultuous time, and we have easier access to do others harm.

We live in an anxious world in an anxious time. You may be anxious about something right now. When we look away from God and his Son, we can easily fall into despair. To say that we live in the most racially divided time in our history would be erroneous. But those born in the seventies, eighties, and nineties feel this heavy weight of racial division. Everything is charged, everything is shared, and everything is being exposed.

My focus here is on race, but you could easily substitute politics or a host of other divisive topics in our culture and see a similar divide and vitriol. What's been the hardest, perhaps, is the hurt associated with people you know who have expressed things you never knew they believed. I also know that the divide and the pain are found not only out there in the world but also right here in the church.

In a recent interview about race, I was asked how I practice self-care so as not to burn out and to be encouraged. My answer was simple: I stop. I stop thinking about the issues for a moment. I don't forget them, and I don't pretend they don't exist. But there comes a time when, in order to have true and lasting peace, we have to understand that we were never meant to carry burdens. Taking captive our thoughts is a means of caring for our souls. I don't do this perfectly—and I never will. But stopping is a practice that reminds me that I'm not God. He desires to carry all the things that keep my mind spinning. And sooner rather than later, the spinning stops, and there's peace. I'm given the grace to think clearly, and I remember God.

TAKE HEART

Paul was no stranger to trials and tribulations; one stop in Lystra almost ended his life. While he was there, the Jews—the very people he once belonged to—gathered a crowd and stoned him for preaching the gospel. After dragging him out of the city, assuming he was dead, they left him there. Paul wasn't dead, and he went on preaching the gospel with Barnabas, even returning to Lystra.

What was Paul's mission? He had two: (1) to share the gospel and make disciples, and (2) to strengthen the disciples so they may endure. What happened next is recorded in Acts 14:21-23:

> When they had preached the gospel to that city and had made many disciples, they returned to Lystra and to Iconium and to Antioch, strengthening the souls of the disciples, encouraging them to continue in the faith, and saying that through many tribulations we must enter the kingdom of God.

The newly converted Christians needed to be strengthened because they would have tribulation in this world. Paul encouraged them to endure in the faith through it because tribulations are part of being a part of the kingdom. Jesus had warned his disciples of this very thing. He told them, "In the world you will have tribulation. But take heart; I have overcome the world" (Jn 16:33). Troubles are part of the Christian life, but we're instructed to take heart. How do we keep our hearts from being troubled? We believe and trust in God (Jn 14:1).

There seems to be a theme of enduring in the faith. We need to have faith to believe God is who he says he is and will do what he says he'll do. Then we need to rest in this truth. In a world of trouble, you and I fight for our hearts by fixing our eyes on Jesus. To "take heart" means to be encouraged by something or to have peace. This is God's desire for us, that we have peace (Jn 16:33). We can be encouraged in our hearts, knowing that Jesus has overcome the world and nothing, not one thing, can ever separate us from him (Rom 8:37-39). Our security enables us to rest, take heart, have peace, and be assured that Jesus is more powerful than the world.

If you are troubled about many things today, I encourage you to pause and to ask God to clear your mind. There is not a quick fix for deep struggles in the mind, but this attempt to settle the mind will be worth it. Maybe the stopping means retreating even for a moment, not disconnecting from your family or church but from all the other noise. Lay down your phone and turn off the news. God will honor your act of faith as you trust him with your concerns rather than carry them on your own. He is faithful.

We won't see this anxiety-ridden division become whole until Jesus returns. All the chaos and confusion will come to a screeching halt. But are we simply resigned to anxious waiting until that day? What if instead we took our anxiety and turned it into faithful prayer? What if we took our anxiety related to racial division and turned it into faithful preaching, writing, or some other creative form? What if we took our anxiety and turned it into faithful action related to division?

No, we don't wait anxiously. We know the future: in heaven there is no injustice. This knowledge gives us endurance to pray and to rest in Jesus. And we pray that his will be done on this earth as it is in heaven (Mt 6:10). As our Savior taught us to pray, we ask knowing that God hears our prayers. Our hope is not in our prayer, our preaching, or our action. Our hope is in our God. We can rest and trust him. We look to that future grace and the hope of a new heaven and new earth to motivate us to bring heaven to earth now.

Because of this hope, we can have courage and rest. We join David in proclaiming,

> I believe that I shall look upon the goodness of the Lord
> in the land of the living!
> Wait for the Lord;
> be strong, and let your heart take courage;
> wait for the Lord! (Ps 27:13-14)

God is the goodness we look upon: his gracious and consistent character. And because we're looking to the Lord, we can take heart and find courage in all the confusion and pain.

Ultimately we need to trust God for our future. The future doesn't look bright in an anxious world. When we look out at the landscape of our culture, it looks dim. But we who know the Lord look out with different eyes—with hope-filled eyes.

REMEMBER OUR ADVERSARY

When I think about our culture and society and I see the great divides over politics, race, and a host of other things, I'm reminded that we have an adversary who is thrilled by all the confusion. It would do us well to remember that Satan exists and wants to devour us (1 Pet 5:8). All the confusion, suspicion, outrage, and fear has something to do with the sin within us, yes. But it's also because our unity and love for one another as Christians points beyond us to the Son of God. Jesus told his disciples that people would know that they were his—and thus that we are his today—because of our love for one another (Jn 13:35). So, what better thing to seek and destroy than our love.

Satan is not all-powerful. God had the power to cast him out of heaven, and Jesus will ultimately destroy his work (1 Jn 3:8). But Satan has some power, and we're instructed to be watchful and to resist him (1 Pet 5:8-9; Jas 4:7). If we are to endure in our personal walk and in our culture, we need to be discerning and to fight the right fights.

Paul gave us a framework for this fight. Here are his final words in his letter to the church in Ephesus:

> Finally, be strong in the Lord and in the strength of his might. Put on the whole armor of God, that you may be able to stand against the schemes of the devil. For we do not wrestle against flesh and blood, but against the rulers, against the authorities, against the cosmic powers over this present darkness, against the spiritual forces of evil in the heavenly places. (Eph 6:10-12)

The Christian life is fought on the battlefield of spiritual warfare. As Paul wrote, we are not fighting against flesh and blood but against the devil. We resist his scheming and lies by putting on the right armor for the fight. The armor consists of knowledge of God through his Word, righteousness provided by Jesus, faith, power by the Spirit, and prayer (Eph 6:14-17). We put on all that we have in Christ and ask God to help us believe all that he has said.

Satan doesn't want us to believe he exists. He'd prefer for us to think that confusion is simply miscommunication or ignorance or hotheaded people who don't have the ability to engage in conversations well. He would prefer that we look at one another and scream, "You are my enemy," and that we fight each other rather than declare, "We have an enemy," and fight him.

How Satan works can look like a number of things, but I've often seen that it's through my thoughts. I have to work hard not to create scenarios that aren't there or assume the worst in others based on something I may have seen. I have to fight to think true thoughts because Satan plants lies, and I can easily run with a lie as if it were true. For example, if someone says something that I think is insensitive, I can make assumptions about that person and what she thinks about a number of things. I may even respond and react without asking questions first. This can lead to an unnecessary conflict—a war that started in my mind and ended up dividing me from another image bearer.

The accuser wants to whisper lies to you about who you are in Christ. He whispers lies about who God is. He'll tell you that God can't handle what we see and hear and experience in this world. But "He disarmed the rulers and authorities and put them to open shame, by triumphing over them in him" (Col 2:15). Satan is not a threat to our God.

DO GOOD

So how do we fight for truth and love in a world of hurt and rage? One way is to be subversive. We need fighters but not the kind that burn down the nation. We need people willing to keep doing good. Yes, overthrow the culture with good. We need warriors willing to do good to their neighbors—as Jesus commanded us to love our neighbor. This is part of the common good for all of society—for blacks and whites, for men and women, for conservatives and liberals, for citizens and the undocumented. For our friends and our enemies.

Don't grow weary in doing good, if indeed you are doing good (Gal 6:9). Don't let fear cause you to grow faint. Don't lose heart. The world today does indeed look grim, but has there ever been a time when the world didn't look grim after sin came in? If we look back over the course of history, we see the same divide and war and terror that some are experiencing now. Other eras weren't as connected; they couldn't see what was happening two thousand miles away within a second of it occurring. But we know from history that the nations have always raged, governments have always been corrupt, and people have always been divided.

But there is reason for great hope. It isn't hope in you or me or our strength. Or in our ruling authorities. Or in our churches, pastors, or fellow congregants. No, we hope in the faithfulness and power of Christ. And we say with King David, "Some trust in chariots and some in horses, but we trust in the name of the LORD our God" (Ps 20:7).

Lift your weak knees, unless they are bowed down in prayer to the One who saves. God isn't asleep; he's awake and active in our midst. If every person leaves the church and we divide in every way possible, we still have a great mission to go and make disciples of all nations. If every social issue that seems to smack Christian ethics in the face becomes law, we continue to preach the truth in love and serve our neighbors. If a radical religious group begins to persecute the church, we can say with faith, "You can kill the body, but you can't kill the soul" (see Mt 10:28).[2] To endure in our culture, we need the faith that only God can give us. I want to fight the fight of faith with a foundation that is strong and firm and otherworldly.

Yet God is not a genie in a bottle, ready to grant all our wishes. We don't shake a magic ball to learn all that he is doing. We wait and trust. God is always working, whether we recognize it or not.

And one day our faith will become sight. God is not wringing his hands, hoping we get our political act together so things can be fixed. God hasn't given up his rule and authority. You and I can resist anxiety and fear by remembering what is true about God.

We have a different and better allegiance, and it isn't to any ruler or authority on this earth. We must remember that our kingdom is of God and is of heaven. We aren't entrusting ourselves to a wimpy, powerless God. God is also our loving Father, and he invites us to come to him and find rest in our Savior, who died for our fear and anxiety. He is our peace. As Paul wrote, "The Lord is at hand; do not be anxious about anything, but in everything by prayer and supplication with thanksgiving let your requests be made known to God. And the peace of God, which surpasses all understanding, will guard your hearts and your minds in Christ Jesus" (Phil 4:5-7).

In chapter fifteen of the Gospel of Luke, Jesus tells of three lost things: a sheep, a coin, and a boy. Apparently the Savior wanted to make a point about the terror of being misplaced and the sheer joy of being found. Recently I hosted an event with about two hundred good friends and other folks from our community, including children. Somehow in the chaos, the daughter of one of my friends was separated from her mom. When the young girl saw me, she ran toward me, tears rolling down her anxious face. Through sobs she explained that she couldn't find her mother.

I gently asked her if she'd like to stay with me until we found her. Looking up into my face and gripping my hand tightly, she nodded an anxious yes. Not a minute later, her mom came up and scooped her daughter into her arms. She had never been far away. In fact, she had been only a few feet away. The little lost girl simply couldn't see her.

We can relate to this little girl. There are moments when the cares of our hearts, our sorrows, and our burdens cause us to wonder where God is. We feel lost and alone. Abandoned. And like that tearful child, we go searching for help in other places. The girl found a good and safe place—a friend to comfort her— but that friend was no replacement for the real thing. She needed her mother.

We read in the psalms that "God is our refuge and strength, a very present help in trouble" (Ps 46:1). Some translations say

God is an "ever-present help." This means God isn't sort-of present, halfway present, distracted, or distant. He is always present. God is with us in our lostness and trouble.

Over the years I've noticed something about fear, sorrow, and trouble. If I'm not vigilant to speak this truth found in Psalm 46 to my heart and mind, trials have the potential to cloud my vision. If I'm worried and anxious, I may not be able to remember where my help comes from. As pastor Anthony Carter wrote,

> By the precious blood of Christ, we belong to Him. Consequently the promise and hope for the Christian is not that there will not be bad days. Indeed, trial is eventually the portion of all born into the world (Job 14:1). Yet, if we are born of God the comfort is that the Lord, who holds the world, holds us, too.[3]

In a society where voices are loud and it feels like chaos reigns, we need to find a refuge in the God who holds us.

Like the little girl, I can anxiously search and wander around, forgetting that my Help is right there beside me. Of course, God isn't physically present. We can't touch him or hold his hand. But he is there just the same, guiding our steps and counseling our hearts according to truth, if we'll only listen.

KNOW WHERE YOU'RE RUNNING

So, what are you running to? Who or what is your refuge? You may run to food as your comfort. Or cling to a substance like alcohol. Or you hope entertainment will drown out your sorrows. In the end, these things leave us empty and longing.

Often we're more empty and longing more deeply than we were at the beginning of our search.

You may take refuge in your friends. To be sure, friends are a gift from the Lord, and each of us ought to pray for safe, reliable, godly friends. Friends encourage and comfort, and the best of them speak the truth in love to us. But they are not a substitute for God, our good and faithful Shepherd. Though they may try, friends can't carry the full weight of our burdens. They can't keep us secure. And even the most reliable friend can't be there at all times. Friends are a gift from God but a wholly inadequate substitute for him.

When I'm struggling and sorrowful, the security of my heavenly Father isn't always the first place I run. I may run to a friend or to my husband. I wish that weren't true, but it is.

It has taken some practice to begin to run to the right place. And I imagine I'm not alone. My hope for you and me is that we train ourselves to remember the Lord who is our true refuge and only hope. The world will not tell us this. And remembering this helps us as we fight the good fight of faith. It helps us put on the armor of God. It helps us endure when the world seems to be set on fire. Hope in God. Run to God.

But this training of our mind takes something outside ourselves: it takes supernatural faith. It takes the same faith to believe that God is the God of salvation and also to believe God is sovereign, omnipotent, good, and eager to be our refuge. Of course, our problem with running to the wrong places is a faith problem. At times we must confess and call out to God like the father crying out to Jesus, "I believe; help my unbelief!"

(Mk 9:24). God is our refuge. There is no substitute for the Almighty in our trouble.

You and I are going to get this wrong again and again. We're going to turn our anxious thoughts to inadequate things to give us security. We're going to be tempted to lean on our own understanding. That's because we have a battle with sin. But God, being rich in mercy, has given us a way of escape through his Son. And God doesn't condemn us for our weakness; instead he invites us to come to him.

So in response to his kind invitation, I resolve to run first to my Father, who invites me to do so in my weakness, in my time of need, in my sorrows. Would you resolve to do the same? God is our refuge; he is our strength.

FAITHFUL IN TIMES OF TROUBLE

When I think of people who had everything stacked against them yet finished their race, faithfully proclaiming and believing in the gospel, John Perkins is one of them. A few years ago, I had the honor of interviewing Perkins about his life, ministry, and work as a civil rights leader.

Dr. Perkins was born into poverty in 1930 and lost his mother to pellagra caused by starvation. He grew up in Mississippi with his grandmother and various family members. His brother served in the military but upon his return to Mississippi was fatally shot by a police officer. After this tragic event, Perkins fled to Southern California, where he eventually became a Christian.

Upon his conversion, Perkins knew he could stay in California and be comfortable, but he felt a call to move back to Mississippi to help the community where he once lived. He said,

> I couldn't be happy anymore with some of the success I got, I felt God calling me back to Mississippi, not as a civil rights worker. I went back there to proclaim this gospel that had so transformed my life. But when I got back there in 1960 of course the Civil Rights Movement was just coming. . . . Any civilized black was longing for the day that they'd be freed from slavery, so I didn't have a choice. It wasn't a choice for a black person growing up in poverty, losing his brother, working for 14 cents a day.[4]

That was the beginning of a lifelong ministry telling Bible stories to kids, working in the community, starting an organization, and writing numerous books.

Dr. Perkins continues to minister to this day, recently publishing a book on race.[5] He is an example of perseverance in work for the common good, shored up by the gospel of Jesus Christ. I'm confident that he grew weary from doing good, but he has not been defeated. You and I can ask the Lord for the endurance and strength to not grow weary in doing good in a world that is raging. He will surely do it.

THE HEART NEEDED,
THE STRENGTH SUPPLIED

Many high school athletes dream of making it into the big leagues: collegiate sports. Scholarships and glory and instant friendships await the college athlete. For some seventeen- and eighteen-year-olds, the anticipation and possibilities are thrilling.

That wasn't me.

I was a very competitive and skilled track athlete, but I lacked one key characteristic: heart. I loved the sport. It was fun. But by my senior year I could tell I was just going through the motions. I was one of the best in the state and had the potential to run for a small college, at the very least. But I lacked the desire to work hard for it. I had other interests and other opportunities. It boiled down to me being too lazy to work hard enough to keep going. I don't beat myself up for this. No regrets! I simply lacked the interest, tenacity, perseverance, and desire to keep going.

We all face limitations, whether physical, mental, volitional, or other, so not all of us have the ability or capacity to be competitive athletes. Like me, most of us aren't called to it.

Yet a race run well isn't attempted in a haphazard manner. Some disciplines and priorities should mark our lives—not because we're attempting to earn something we don't already have but because we're compelled to live in a new way.

Athletes discipline themselves to compete at a high level and to win. Whatever their sport, it requires tenacity, perseverance, faithfulness, and intentionality. In a similar way, as we embark on the disciplines of the Christian life, we ought to consider if we're running in a flippant or haphazard manner and how that's affecting what we believe about God and our daily lives. But it's hard to pursue what we don't desire.

My lack of pursuit of collegiate sports was partly because I didn't want to do it. It was the Lord's doing, as I wasn't called to that vocation. All the sweat necessary to make myself a better athlete—well, it just wasn't worth it to me. In a similar way, it's hard to keep running the race of faith if Christ isn't worth it to you. If he is only a slogan or a nice guy, he won't be enough to endure for. You and I have to fight to remember Jesus in order to desire him.

And here's the really good news: unlike the athlete who must dig deep to finish her race, our race requires tapping into the strength of another. As the psalmist cried out, "My flesh and my heart may fail, but God is the strength of my heart and my portion forever" (Ps 73:26). We won't always have the heart to endure. We won't always be eager to keep going, and our heart will fail us if this life is all about us.

But it isn't all about us. It's all about him. And because it's about him, we fight to remember.

KING DAVID'S STRUGGLE

I wonder if King David wrestled similarly. In the first few verses of Psalm 103, he teaches us how to remember the Lord by telling his soul to bless the Lord. To bless the Lord is to sing his praises. We aren't merely to read about God; our soul needs to praise him, thank him, and exult him. We need to remind our soul daily to delight in the Lord.

Any relationship that's of any value takes intentionality. And so we must be intentional in our relationship with the Lord. This means we need to remind ourselves why we delight in and enjoy God. We need to "forget not all his benefits" (Ps 103:2).

This call to bless the Lord isn't just for our mouth; it engages all of us—"all that is within me" (Ps 103:1). David's worship in this psalm reminds me of Jesus' command for us to love the Lord with all our heart, soul, and mind. Nothing is left unaffected by him. We are to love him with everything that's within us. Every part of us ought to bless the Lord. He is holy and deserves our full attention and admiration. So with intentionality we remind our souls and our hearts and our minds to bless his holy name.

David also preached to his soul not to forget the Lord's benefits. This reminder is not only for times of discouragement and sorrows. Regardless of the season of life we're in, we should always remember the work of the Lord on our behalf. When we're discouraged, there's a temptation to forget his goodness. In times of temptation, we must remind ourselves of all he has done. But we're most tempted to forget the benefits of the Lord when we're experiencing abundance, when we think we have all we need. We forget we can do nothing apart from the

Lord (Jn 15:5). Let's resist the urge to remember the Lord only when feeling desperate. Let's take the following three steps.

Praise the Lord that he forgives all of your iniquity (Ps 103:3). He doesn't forgive in part; he forgives completely. Every sinful thought and deed has been purchased on the cross of Christ. We don't deserve his forgiveness. We sent him to the cross. Oh that this truth may send us singing blessings to the Lord! Jesus paid the price we could not pay. In his mercy and grace, he says to we who have placed our faith and trust in him, "Your sins are forgiven."

Remember that Jesus' death and resurrection defeated death. So much of our discouragement and worry come as a result of failing or difficult health or experiencing the pain of a friend or loved one. But one day, every disease will be healed. No more sickness, no more pain. No more arthritis. No more cancer. The diseases that have plagued us since the fall will be eradicated. What an awesome benefit of knowing the Lord. When we're weary of sickness, it's good to remind our soul that one day all that is within us will be healed.

Remind our souls of our salvation. No matter your story, whether saved as a young child or while steeped in sin, God has redeemed your life from the pit. We were helpless and dead to our sins, whether we realized it or not. We were all hell-bound without the Lord's intervention. The radical transformation in our hearts means we have been forever changed by amazing mercy and grace. He crowns us with his steadfast, never-changing, everlasting love and mercy.

Bless the Lord, oh my soul! For all eternity we will be discovering the benefits of the Lord. Today let's remember the Lord.

If we truly love others, we think about them, study them, and reflect on the good and wonderful aspects of their character. It isn't selfish to remember when someone has done great things for you. If we make such an effort with other people, we ought to pursue the Lord the same way. Bless the Lord, soul. Don't be forgetful in discouragement, anxiety, or abundant blessing. Remember to praise him for his benefits today, tomorrow, and every day. And even if we forget, God is deeply invested in us, in his mission, and in his Son. He is pursuing us with such irresistible grace, we aren't able to fight off his love and keeping power.

I want to long for Jesus. I want to desire to know him. You and I need daily help and transformation so that our running toward Jesus doesn't become another task to check off a list. Jesus is everything. He is better than all other things.

HAVING A HEART FOR JESUS

Okay, okay, okay. Jesus is everything. Sure. We know all this to be true, but how do we keep it ever before us? How does it become something more than just words? If my running requires heart, where does that come from? Our answer is back in the Psalms. Let's read more:

> When my soul was embittered,
>   when I was pricked in heart,
> I was brutish and ignorant;
>   I was like a beast toward you.
>
> Nevertheless, I am continually with you;
>   you hold my right hand.

You guide me with your counsel,
  and afterward you will receive me to glory.
Whom have I in heaven but you?
  And there is nothing on earth that I desire
  besides you.
My flesh and my heart may fail,
  but God is the strength of my heart and my portion
  forever. (Ps 73:21-26)

The psalmist was grieving and envious. He had become em-
bittered and had sinned against God. He was brutish. But we
see a merciful word: *nevertheless*. The psalmist had not acted
rightly; his heart was far from the Lord. Nevertheless God was
always with him. God was continually holding him. It's the
same for you and me. We have sinned. We aren't always faithful.
Nevertheless God is with us to the end of time—and beyond.
In our inability to hold on to him, he is ever holding on to us.

As we see in this psalm, God will guide us with his counsel—
with his Word. In moments when we lack the strength to lift
our heads, when we feel we can't keep going, we look to the
promises and character of God found in the pages of Scripture.
And we remember that God has always been faithful and true
to his word.

Practically, this is like preaching to ourselves minute by
minute. I can get up in the morning and spend time with the
Lord, but I struggle to live out the truth I read if I'm not reminding myself constantly of the goodness and character of
our Father God. Maybe that's one reason we are told to pray
without ceasing (1 Thess 5:17), to be ever engaged with our

Lord so that when we begin to forget because of a new circumstance or anxiety or fear, we can remember him.

In understanding who our God is, we can say, "Whom have I in heaven but you" (Ps 73:25). There's nothing and no one who compares to our God. And this truth provides strength to our hearts. Our flesh may fail, our hearts may fail, but we will endure because God is the strength of our heart. David sang a similar song:

Blessed be the LORD!
For he has heard the voice of my pleas for mercy.
The LORD is my strength and my shield;
in him my heart trusts, and I am helped;
my heart exults,
and with my song I give thanks to him. (Ps 28:6-7)

How could David's heart trust, and how could he so confidently proclaim that God was his strength? Because he was confident in God's promises to protect him. God is our strength because we know who he is, and he cannot go against himself. What are some promises you can tell yourself today to strengthen your heart for tomorrow? Write them down. Ask the God who hears to answer you in your distress or in the mundane or even in your joy, so you don't forget where your strength comes from.

One danger is that we think about perseverance and a need for strength only when we're experiencing a trial. The Christian life isn't rainbows and sunshine all the time, but it isn't always drudgery either. Often it's more like waking up and doing the next ordinary thing.

Maybe for you enduring looks like a quiet life (1 Thess 4:10-12). Your day-to-day looks like minding and tending to your business, working with your hands, doing the most ordinary things every single day to the glory of God.

My friend Linda understands the struggle to find strength in God in the ordinary. She has been a Christian for forty-four years and has lived what many would call an ordered and ordinary life as a pastor's wife for much of those years. Linda shares her insights:

> I believe it has often been easier for me to endure in a Christlike way when going through major trials than through day-to-day matters. Not only does it seem easier to see that major trials are part of his sovereign plan for my life, but I can also recognize that since I have no control over whatever the situation and its subsequent outcome is, I not only can trust him, but I really want to trust him, and I desperately want to know his plan for me. I find myself being able to focus on the absolute truth that he is good, and he will always do good for me.
>
> Where I struggle to endure in a Christlike way is in my day-to-day life, especially when I am disappointed or my expectations haven't been met. I know that if I am going to have day-to-day Christlike endurance, it must be fueled by having an intimate relationship with him. This kind of intimacy cannot truly exist without spending time daily in his Word and prayer. Knowing him is what allows me to endure, especially in times when trusting, surrendering, and obedience seem difficult (James 1:2-4).

Yes, Linda, knowing him allows for our enduring. The Christian life isn't easy, but it isn't necessarily a life of constant suffering, sorrows, and pain either. In the mundane, ordinary times, we might be tempted to trust in our own strength and forget God. All of our life—every minute—is about him. We sing that old song, "I Need Thee Every Hour."

While studying what Scripture says about endurance, I found the word *abiding*. A heart that endures and is strengthened by God is also a heart that abides. *Abiding* means to dwell or continue in. It's lasting, perpetual. To continue, we must abide.

LEARNING TO ABIDE

Interestingly I hear the words "abide in Christ" mentioned a lot by women as a way to express rest. At least I think that's what they mean. The truth is, I've never had the phrase defined for me clearly, though I've heard it shared often. To gain more understanding, I started digging into God's Word to see what he says about abiding in Christ.

Jesus gave a series of farewell addresses that are recorded in John 13–17. He knew that he would soon be lifeless on a tree—the crucified King. And in the middle of it all, he graciously reminded us that to be his means to bear fruit; we bear fruit by abiding in him, remaining in him.

Jesus described himself as the true vine and his Father as the vinedresser (Jn 15:1-11). The idea of the true vine was a way to contrast Jesus with Old Testament Israel. The hearers would understand that he was saying that he was the Messiah and the fulfillment of the covenant because of the Old Testament references to a vineyard (Is 5:1-7; 27:2-6).

He explained that branches that don't bear fruit are taken away, but branches that bear fruit are pruned to bear more fruit. To "bear fruit" simply means to grow in character—to become more like Christ and to reflect the fruit of the Spirit (Gal 5:22-23).

This is where we come to his command to abide: "Abide in me, and I in you. As the branch cannot bear fruit by itself, unless it abides in the vine, neither can you, unless you abide in me" (Jn 15:4).

Before Jesus got to the meaning of abiding, he showed what it looks like *not* to abide in him: "If anyone does not abide in me he is thrown away like a branch and withers, and the branches are gathered, thrown into the fire, and burned" (Jn 15:6).

I guess I'm what you would call a plant killer. I purchase plants and try to care for them, but I often fail miserably. I forget to water them, choking them from their needed nourishment. Then one day I turn around, and there they are, withered away. This didn't happen overnight; it happened after a period of neglect. One by one, the branches (or leaves) fell off the vine.

This is what Jesus explained to us in John 15:4-6. When we don't abide in him, we are like my pitiful plants. Our roots don't go deep, so we never receive nourishment. It's as if we were never truly planted. The fruit of the vine is proof of our faith—not perfection but fruit.

Not until John 15:10 do we get a picture of what it looks like to abide in Jesus: "If you keep my commandments, you will abide in my love, just as I have kept my Father's commandments and abide in his love." To abide in Jesus means to keep his commandments, and to keep his commandments means to love God with all our hearts and souls and minds and to love our neighbors as ourselves (Mt 22:37-39). One way we display our love for God is through our trust, prayer, and devotion to him. We continue with him. We abide through relationship. We pursue in love. We pray in love. We obey in love.

And here is the good news: "We love because he first loved us" (1 Jn 4:19). We didn't choose him; he chose us to walk out our faith in obedience to him (Jn 15:16). Apart from Christ, we can't do anything (Jn 15:5). This is good news to the weary person who thinks she must muster up strength to pursue and know Christ and to love her neighbor—a fruit Jesus emphasized. He provides the grace and the strength.

The fruit Jesus speaks of is simply evidence of a relationship with him. It is the result of a relationship that he initiated through and by his sovereign love. Jesus reminded us that there is no greater love than someone laying down his life for his friends. He then added, "You are my friends if you do what I command you" (Jn 15:14).

Let that soak in for a minute. We are his friends if we obey his command to love, and that command is fulfilled through abiding. As we abide in him, we bear the fruit of righteousness. This doesn't add to our salvation, which is by grace alone through faith alone, yet it confirms our transformed heart. And the offer to be Jesus' friend—yes, a friend of the author and perfecter of our faith, the Alpha and Omega, the beautiful One, the one who bore our sins and transgression—is irresistible for Christians.

Abide in him, and he will abide in you. He who began a good work in you will complete it (Phil 1:6). "He who calls you is faithful; he will surely do it" (1 Thess 5:24).[1]

TALES OF ABIDING

Abiding takes different forms depending on our stage of life and our context. For Jennifer, abiding meant committing to her dorm Bible study, and the fruit was a renewed desire for the Word of God. She also found sisters who sustained her and prayed for her throughout the semester. For Juanita, abiding in Christ gave her the courage to escape an abusive boyfriend and find refuge in a protective church community. For Jung-an, abiding meant persevering in her mission work for long years when there seemed to be no fruit. All of these women stayed close to Jesus through whatever circumstance they endured.

Abiding also looks like the trust we see in Sister Kelly, a washerwoman in Nashville after the Civil War. She participated in gatherings of slaves for singing and praying. Here's what she said in an oral interview after her husband's death: "What is written of trouble on the heart is written in His blood, and nobody can take the glory of His name away from you. He sho' guides my trembling feet, I tell you, bless His holy name; He sho' is my heavenly Father, ooh merciful God."[2]

Sister Kelly had lost much, but she had everything she needed in the Father. She dwelled in the presence of the Lord. He was all she had. She continued with him till the end. I pray for that kind of faith and rest in God. Everything I need is in God—nothing more, nothing less.

TAKING STEPS IN
PRACTICAL DISCIPLINES

My love for physical fitness began when I was a young child, as I adored my father's presence and involvement. He would do things like race me in the parking lot and cheer me on in races on the track. This grew into a lifelong love of sports, including gymnastics, dance, track and field, cheerleading, cycling, and more.

When I became a Christian at twenty-two, I discovered a new dimension to my favorite activities. Paul wrote, "For while bodily training is of some value, godliness is of value in every way, as it holds promise for the present life and also for the life to come" (1 Tim 4:8). As he advised Christians to be trained in good doctrine and discernment, he knew it required diligence and effort—as does physical training.

We have become a nation of athletic hobbyists: runners, cyclists, yogis, and CrossFit devotees. About half of US adults meet current federal guidelines for aerobic activity.[1] That may not seem like a lot, but it's the highest figure on record. Millions of kids play organized sports, so much that the question hasn't become if your kid will participate but in which sports. Over the past several years, my kindergartner has been thrilled to don pink shin guards for soccer, and my boy has ventured into the world of small shorts and long runs for cross-country.

We're right to be concerned about what happens when our love of fitness gets taken to extremes—over-exercise, high pressure, intense competition—and the church should continue to caution us against any hobby becoming an idol. But before we roll our eyes about another fitness challenge or workout of the day a friend posts on Facebook, we would do well to celebrate what our growing embrace of physical activity gets right.

As a seasoned fitness professional, I can tell you that there are many benefits of exercise: a healthier body, a happier mood, clearer thoughts, deeper sleep, and more. But there are also spiritual benefits. As fitness continues to carve a greater space in our daily routines and our cultural discourse, there's a potential for Christians to better appreciate our God-given bodies, our efforts, and God's creation. The disciplines involved in exercise are similar to those we have in the Christian life. In both, we need to build endurance to finish the race.

Soon after my conversion, I began to couple my love of fitness with a new purpose. This was magnified after I had my son and realized that my body would never be the same. But God turned any anxiety over stretch marks or post-baby weight into excitement to see how he would use me in new ways as I trained.

God is gracious to allow us to enjoy exercise while here on earth. As I was growing up, fitness was centered on me—on how I felt and how I performed. Now I realize that I can bring God glory, enjoy him and his creation, and serve my family well while enjoying the physical activities themselves.

God uses the idea of training, running a race, and enduring as a way to direct our attention to our faith (Is 40:31; Heb 12:1; 2 Tim 4:7). It's no surprise that physical activity reminds me of the race set before me and of God's goodness in it.

During my bike rides, I find myself appreciating God in new ways. When I ride through a greenway and look at the bright yellow flowers lining the paths, spot a rare white squirrel in our local park, or dodge a baby snake scurrying across my path, I know there is a God. His creation calls out his name, and it is glorious. He has made a world for us to enjoy, subdue, and care for (Gen 1:28-31).[2]

RUN FOR THE PRIZE

Paul must have understood that the race analogy reaches into the depths of who we are and what we can relate to. In 1 Corinthians 9, we see him challenging the Corinthians to consider their brothers and sisters, who were struggling to give up their rights on behalf of those around them. They didn't want to sacrifice their desires for the sake of others. But Paul was willing to do whatever it took to win people to Christ (1 Cor 9:23).

He challenged them by writing, "Do you not know that in a race all the runners run, but only one receives the prize? So run that you may obtain it. Every athlete exercises self-control in all things. They do it to receive a perishable wreath, but we an imperishable" (1 Cor 9:24-25). We'll dive into these verses in the final chapter of this book, but take notice now that Paul used the example of a runner who disciplines his body to run the race well. Paul's point is that if we discipline ourselves for something perishable, we ought to discipline our bodies all the more, for we have an imperishable reward.

There are many books about work, self-discipline, and effectiveness, just as there are numerous apps and resources for exercising. At the beginning of each year, the sales of self-help books and devices go into full swing as we set goals for exercise, waking up early, and other disciplines. But here Paul tells us that we need to discipline our bodies for more than fitness and work. We need to run the race with endurance and discipline our bodies for godliness (1 Cor 9:27).

The race set before us requires tenacity in the spiritual disciplines. These disciplines aren't meant to be added to-dos, and they most definitely aren't the way to gain a seat at the Lord's table. They're meant to help us finish well and enjoy the Lord. Disciplines enable us to put on the whole armor of God, which includes reading, praying, and communing with the Lord by reminding ourselves of the gospel and our faith (Eph 6:10-20). We don't have to be superhuman Christians to finish well. We don't need a seminary degree, although that's fine and acceptable. We do need to read and meditate on God's Word and to pray. That alone takes a great deal of discipline in our busy and connected world.

Because of this, I'll begin with two areas that the Word speaks of often and that are—in my estimation—the most important but neglected in the Christian life: studying God's Word and prayer.

THE GIFT OF GOD'S WORD

Ponder for a moment how amazing it is that God's Word has endured these thousands of years to become the most loved, hated, and misused book ever written. It has been destroyed and outlawed in places throughout history, and yet the words of God on its pages continue to live on. Within its pages are words like "I am the way, and the truth, and the life" (Jn 14:6), "you shall have no other gods before me" (Ex 20:3), and "to all who did receive him, who believed in his name, he gave the right to become children of God" (Jn 1:12). These indicate that a true believer would proclaim Christ as the only way to salvation.

And yet we so often run to other things. As I scroll through a social-media feed, I glance at the one-liners and wonder, "Does that apply to me?" I click on an article that piques my interest and ask, "Is this something I should take to heart, or is it bad advice?" And so on.

Every day we are inundated with articles and posts telling us how we ought to think and live and be. Many of the thoughts in them are well-meaning, and some are universally true. But if we aren't careful and discerning, we can rely too much on the words of those outside our community—or, even worse, rely on the words of others over the words of our Father. That's one of many reasons we need to be disciplined to read God's Word. Saying no to social media isn't typically listed as a spiritual discipline, but to practice any discipline we need to learn to unplug.

People searching for answers have always been on the lookout for the latest and greatest advice on how to live. And the advice is out there—everywhere! The self-help sections of bookstores are well stocked with new and innovative ideas. There's advice (good and bad) in articles, on TV, and on radio. In the age of the internet, we no longer need to go searching far.

Advice is in our faces at all times—that is, whenever we pick up our smartphones. And many of us, if we're honest, spend several hours doing that every day. As a result, we need to be even more diligent about what we believe, think, and dwell on.

The apostle Paul understood the importance of fighting the right battles with the right tools: "For the weapons of our warfare are not of the flesh but have divine power to destroy strongholds. We destroy arguments and every lofty opinion raised against the knowledge of God, and take every thought captive to obey Christ, being ready to punish every disobedience, when your obedience is complete" (2 Cor 10:4-6).

In this battle for our minds (a battle I know all too well), our first line of defense is the Word of God. Every opinion, every article, every social-media post, and even this book needs to be weighed against the knowledge of God. That may seem extreme, but the cost of believing the wrong thing is too great to risk doing otherwise. However, we can't have a knowledge of God without seeking him, and one of the primary ways we seek God is through his Word. If we believe—truly believe—that the Bible is God-breathed (2 Tim 3:16), then no book, no article, no social media words of wisdom can compare to the Word, which teaches us about our Savior, corrects our hearts, and trains us in righteousness.

It's tempting to run to other sources—even good resources—to give us what only God's Word is equipped to do. The Bible is inerrant, so everything else should be weighed against it.

The psalmists, in particular, focused on running to the Lord and meditating on his words day and night. (See Psalm 1:1-3; 16:8; 19:14; 104:34; and 119:15-16 just for starters.) If we want to grow in discernment, we will fill ourselves with the truth of God's Word. We can't fight a battle without preparing for it. We must train our brains to be able to sift through the noise.

The solution is too easy, really. We don't necessarily need to retreat from social media, and we definitely don't want to stop reading books. These tools can be a gift that points us back to our Savior. But they are not the Word, and they can't replace the Word.

So delight in the law of the Lord day and night (Ps 1:2). Read the Bible regularly. Memorize verses about the character of God. Train your mind to discern what is true, pure, lovely, and admirable—and think about those things (Phil 4:8). Be ready to speak God's truth to your heart and mind because you've already stored it up in your heart.

Getting in the Word of God can take many forms. I tend to read the Bible daily and to study and meditate on certain passages, depending on the week. Meditation may look like reading and rewriting the passage so I'm able to articulate what the passage is saying. Or it may be fixating on one word. For me, study often means using a system in which I observe (read the text), interpret it (using cross-referencing, etc.), and apply it to my life.

Others believe that everyday Bible reading isn't necessary. Rather, taking one day to dissect the Word as much as possible is the best method. This person would do most of the methods I would but maybe spend a little longer in the one-day study, which would be great for a day of rest.

There are other ways to cement the Word in our hearts and minds as well: Bible memorization, praying verses, posting verses in rooms we visit frequently, and many others. The point is to study, read, and meditate on one of the greatest gifts from our Lord: his very words to us.

DELIGHTING IN PRAYER

Praying is never an overreaction.

It's not always our first reaction. Paul, inspired by the Holy Spirit, commanded that believers do this:

> Rejoice in the Lord always; again I will say, rejoice. Let your reasonableness be known to everyone. The Lord is at hand; do not be anxious about anything, but in every-thing by prayer and supplication with thanksgiving let your requests be made known to God. And the peace of God, which surpasses all understanding, will guard your hearts and your minds in Christ Jesus. (Phil 4:4-7)

A major theme in the book of Philippians is joy, and the driving force that enables us to maintain joy is prayer. We are exhorted to replace our anxieties with prayer and supplication (humbly and earnestly asking). And then God, who is the great giver of all good things, provides for us joy and peace. What a generous God!

So we pray our one prayer, we receive immediate peace and joy, and we move along. Right? I don't think so. Perhaps that's why Paul told the Thessalonians to "rejoice always, pray without ceasing" (1 Thess 5:16-17). Unceasing prayer means that our minds are continually engaged with and in communion with the Lord. Why might we need to do this? Because we forget quickly and easily. We forget that God is in control and that we can trust him the moment we proclaim it.

My morning time with the Lord is how I prefer to start my day. It centers me on the gospel and gives me a right frame of mind before I step into the busyness and demands of the day. It's easy to have peace and joy in the quietness of the morning, sitting with a cup of coffee while everyone else in the house is asleep. But I need God every hour! Prayer is an act of war; it's taking up our arms against the lies of the evil one and entrusting ourselves to our mighty Savior.

Perhaps the greatest motivation for us to pray is that we get to. We have access to the Holy One. We have access to the Father. This knowledge is too great for me! I can't fully grasp it, but I can enjoy it. Jesus made a way for us to speak to the Lord of the universe (Eph 2:18). And because of Jesus, we aren't approaching a holy God to be annihilated. We have access to approach the throne of grace to receive mercy and help in our time of need (Heb 4:16).

So why would we not pray? I don't ask that self-righteously; I'm asking myself too. If I truly believe all of this to be true, why would I ever rely on my own strength and wisdom? Why would I ever worry when I have access to the good God who controls all things? What this boils down to is that you and I may struggle with doubt more than we realize.

It's not that we don't believe. We do believe. It's that we don't believe enough, or we doubt that prayer works, or we wonder if God truly hears and acts. Comically, to fight our doubts we must run to the Lord with them. James wrote about doubts, saying,

If any of you lacks wisdom, let him ask God, who gives generously to all without reproach, and it will be given him. But let him ask in faith, with no doubting, for the one who doubts is like a wave of the sea that is driven and tossed by the wind. For that person must not suppose that he will receive anything from the Lord; he is a double-minded man, unstable in all his ways. (Jas 1:5-8)

James never quite minces words, does he? His strong analogy is meant to drive us toward God with our doubts and away from the world. His picture of a man in the sea being tossed back and forth by waves is instructive. When we doubt, we are double-minded, tossed back and forth between what we know to be true and what the world, the devil, or our fears tell us is true. When you and I doubt, we operate as one who has two minds, so to speak, which is unstable.

We are going to doubt from time to time, but it's important that we take our doubts to the Lord, confess, and ask for grace to believe.

Another motivator is to remember that Jesus is interceding for us. The writer of Hebrews tells us, "Consequently, he is able to save to the uttermost those who draw near to God through him, since he always lives to make intercession for them" (Heb 7:25). Jesus lives! Jesus is alive right now, praying for you. He is interceding on your behalf before the Father (Rom 8:34). Jesus died but death could not keep him. Jesus rose and defeated death, and he now lives to continually speak for you and me. If that's not amazing grace, I don't know what is.

Your prayer time doesn't have to be anything elaborate, but I'm praying that, for you and me, it will be consistent and honest— every day. As African pastor Conrad Mbewe wrote, "This relationship with God is too important not to take it seriously—you must come to God with honest lips (Psalm 145:18)."[3] We don't need fancy words; we need desperate hearts.

PRAYER FOR BEGINNERS

Some things just seem easier to learn as a kid. Whether it's how to swim or ski or speak a new language, kids seem to absorb new skills quickly and naturally. I learned how to use a Hula-Hoop, dance, and ride a bike as a kid, but one thing I didn't learn was how to pray.

I became a Christian at twenty-two. The woman who first shared the gospel with me told me she had several friends praying that I would come to know the Lord. The day I made that commitment, three friends gathered around me and joined me in praying to the Lord for the forgiveness of my sin. But I still needed to learn how to pray. And prayer didn't come naturally for me.

Maybe you are a new Christian or you haven't ever committed yourself to prayer. Or maybe prayer has been odd to you; you can't see God, and you wonder if he's really there, actually hearing you? Of course, the greatest benefit of prayer is communion with God. But I remember feeling the newness of it and having questions about it. Even Jesus didn't assume we'd understand how to pray; he graciously taught his followers in his Sermon on the Mount (Mt 6:5-15). Everything in the Christian life is a process, including learning disciplines like prayer. So you and I can grow in our prayer lives.

As you begin your journey into praying, I'm tempted to give you a big to-do list. Instead I'd like to suggest two things that have helped me and continue to assist me in my pursuit of God through prayer.

1. Remember the who. In Matthew 6, Jesus taught his disciples how to pray by giving them the Lord's Prayer. God is holy and awesome in every way, and yet he is also our Father, who not only allows us to speak to him but also invites us to. God asks us to draw near to his throne of grace (Heb 4:16). We are praying to the one who is described as a rock (1 Sam 2:2), all-knowing (Is 40:13-14), and all-powerful (Lk 1:37). God is greater than our hearts and minds can begin to imagine—and yet he is mindful of us (Ps 8:4). God loves us with an everlasting love—so much so that he gave his Son for us (Jn 3:16).

This is only a taste of who our God, our Father, is. Remember *who* he is, and let it motivate you to run to him in prayer.

2. Go and pray. As I've been teaching my kids to pray, they often respond with "Mommy, I don't know how." In helping them understand how to pray, I could teach them the Lord's Prayer (and I will), but I've decided to start even more basic: I ask them simply to speak. I tell them they can talk to God.

I wouldn't reserve this advice for children. You and I can benefit from simply opening our mouths and speaking to God. We don't need to overcomplicate it. We need to speak, ask, beg, cry, thank, and plead. He is listening! Our prayers need not be complicated or have lofty words. As a matter of fact, Jesus specifically told us God isn't impressed with that (Mt 6:7). We can be real, honest, and humble before him.

Practically, you can grab a friend and ask her to begin to pray with you as a way to learn to pray. I remember meeting with my two girlfriends every other week for several years after I first became a Christian. We shared about the various trials and joys we were experiencing and prayed each time.

Something else to try is memorizing the Lord's Prayer and reciting it back to the Lord, or opening to the psalms and praying through those as a guide, or writing your prayers in a journal. It's been eighteen years since I started my first wobbly attempts at praying, and I'm still learning and growing in my prayer life. I find it to be one of the sweetest ways to commune with my Father. God invites me to come to him day or night, any time I need to. And honestly I sometimes still stumble over my words. I'm thankful that in my weakness, when I don't know what to say, the Lord knows and the Spirit intercedes for me (Rom 8:26).

Most of all, God longs to hear our prayers: "Before they call I will answer; while they are yet speaking I will hear" (Is 65:24). Pray, for he is listening.

SEEKING SOLITUDE

Bible reading and prayer are generally listed at the top of the spiritual disciplines, and rightly so. God has given us these tools to interact directly with him. Let's explore two lesser-known disciplines that give us more of Jesus: solitude and fasting. Let's start with solitude.

I recently prepared to go on my first silent retreat. As a friend told me about her experiences with such retreats, I was filled with both great anticipation and dread. I feared having only the voice in my head speaking loudly to my heart. What would I be thinking? What sorrows had I not faced because I was always engaged in something, with something? I started crying at the thought of being silent for even a day, let alone three.

The noise around me so often shuts out my anxieties, insecurities, fears—and frankly my need for Jesus. In other words, because of constant noise via social media, my lovely home, work, and much more, it's not often that I get extended times to meditate on the Lord and pray.

Like many of us, I spend only about six to eight hours a day in silence—and that's when I'm sleeping. Even when I'm reading God's Word, there's generally someone around, and it's rarely for longer than an hour at a time. This is one of the reasons I've begun exploring the benefits of solitude, of pulling away to be alone with the Lord in thought, prayer, and Bible reading for an extended period. And as with all things related to the Lord, I look to him for guidance.

Jesus knew a thing or two about noise. People were constantly searching for him, hoping he would perform a miracle or teach them. Even those closest to him would wake him up if they needed him (Lk 8:24). Luke recorded a glimpse into Jesus' busy life that's inspiring, encouraging, and instructive to us: A man with leprosy came to Jesus, asking for healing. Jesus healed him and then instructed him not to tell anyone about what had happened. But the healed man didn't keep it to himself. And could you blame him? When Jesus does great things, I want to scream it from the mountaintops too. Jesus' work and fame spread far and wide, and crowds gathered to hear him and be healed (Lk 5:15). But instead of healing or teaching, our Lord "would withdraw to desolate places and pray" (Lk 5:16).

The word *would* indicate that the practice of withdrawal and prayer was Jesus' habit. And the Gospels record other times when the Savior withdrew to pray:

- Jesus got up very early and went to a solitary place (Mk 1:35).

- He went up on a mountainside by himself to pray (Mt 14:23).

- Yet another time he retreated to a mountain (Lk 6:12).

- Likely the most famous scene in Scripture was when Jesus prayed in the Garden of Gethsemane before his crucifixion (Lk 22:44).

The writer of Hebrews reminds us that Jesus prayed many prayers throughout his life on earth (Heb 5:7).

If Jesus needed to withdraw to be with the Father, how much more do we need to do likewise? He needed his Father. He needed time alone to pray and rest. There was a desperation to his prayers, as he uttered loud, anguished cries. Jesus, the God-man, needed communion with the Father. How much more do we need God! How much more do we need to withdraw and spend time alone with him!

As with all things that are practical in nature regarding devotion to our Lord, solitude is not a requirement. It is a benefit and a gift but not necessary for true communion with God. We don't earn anything before the Lord by adding the discipline of solitude. But we likely can agree that without some silence hearing from the Lord through his Word is difficult. And without silence, prayers are easily cluttered by noise. At some point, getting alone even for a little while is important to the Christian walk.

Can you imagine the beauty of sitting quietly with the Lord for an extended period of solitude? He's likely to reveal your most inward parts but only to mend them by his grace and kindness. Think of the uninterrupted Bible meditation—no schedule or task to attend to, nothing but reading and learning and soaking up the wisdom and knowledge of God. It all seems so glorious to me. And to think that we'll be doing this for eternity—sitting at the feet of Jesus, listening, learning, worshiping, and enjoying him forever. I can hear through God's Word him calling to us even now to be still and know that he is God (Ps 46:10).

REMEMBER FASTING?

Along with solitude, fasting is difficult to do and rarely done in contemporary Protestant churches. I hear and see calls to prayer quite often, but I rarely hear a call to fast.

As I write, we are at the beginning of Lent, which hasn't been my church's practice. But I love learning about this time of prayer, repentance, and self-denial. Lent is observed mostly in Anglican, Orthodox, Catholic, Lutheran, and Methodist churches. Beyond the occasional friend sharing a picture of ashes on her forehead and me hearing about others giving up various things for Lent—like chocolate, television, or the internet—I haven't connected with Lent much. I've noticed that sometimes there's not much reverence in the practice. Some people observe Lent without truly knowing why.

Many of us take a similar approach to fasting in general. Do we know why we're fasting, if we fast at all? To evaluate whether fasting is a part of your understanding of Christian disciplines and a generally important part of your community, answer these two questions: (1) When was the last time you fasted? (2) When was the last time you heard a sermon on fasting?

In answering those questions, we see how much we value or do not value fasting. Few of us have heard a sermon on fasting or—much less—actually fasted lately. This is not to add a heavy load or burden. It's to build awareness. Fasting is at the bottom of most of our priority lists, and we aren't commanded in Scripture to fast. Yet it seems that fasting was a normal part of Jesus' routine, so why wouldn't we fast too?

In the Old Testament, fasting was a part of the law—a requirement for Israelites. They were to "afflict" themselves, which meant to humble themselves before the Lord by fasting and praying once a year (Lev 16:29). There is no such commandment in the New Testament, and nowhere do we see a requirement now to fast. Yet in the Sermon on the Mount, Jesus seemed to assume that we would fast and gave us warnings for when we do:

> And when you fast, do not look gloomy like the hypocrites, for they disfigure their faces that their fasting may be seen by others. Truly, I say to you, they have received their reward. But when you fast, anoint your head and wash your face, that your fasting may not be seen by others but by your Father who is in secret. And your Father who sees in secret will reward you. (Mt 6:16-18)

Jesus said that *when* we fast, we are not to look gloomy, indicating that at some point we would indeed practice fasting. His concern, as always, was the heart behind it and not the action of it. So we aren't to seek attention in our spiritual practice of fasting. Jesus also spoke of fasting in private, so when we fast, we need to resist the temptation to draw attention to ourselves. Isn't it beautiful that when we fast alone, we are not actually alone. God is with us, God sees it, and remarkably God rewards it.

Jesus wouldn't ask anything of us that he himself had not endured. He spent forty days and forty nights fasting in the wilderness (Mt 4:1-11). That fast didn't end with a seven-course meal and wine; it ended with him being tempted by Satan. Satan wanted Jesus to fail so he would be disqualified from ministry; Jesus couldn't be the Messiah if he sinned. Of course, Jesus didn't give in to Satan's schemes. He didn't command us to such extraordinary fasting. (Note that Moses fasted for forty days and nights. See Ex 24:18.)

Fasting and prayer are close sisters, often paired and spoken of together as a way to fight temptation and focus on the Lord. In the New Testament, fasting and prayer was often used in preparation for something:

- Before being sent out on mission, the leaders prayed and fasted (Acts 13:1-3).

- People prayed and fasted for guidance and for making decisions (Acts 14:23).

- The disciples did not fast while Jesus was with them, but once he was gone, they fasted in anticipation of his return (Mt 9:14-17).

- And ultimately fasting and prayer is an act of worship, preparing our hearts and minds to praise the Lord, repent, and receive the Lord (Lk 2:37).

Fasting is yet another means to engage with the Lord, deny ourselves, and worship. We can fast from food or media or any other thing that would be a sacrifice to give up. But in everything we do, we must remember the objective of our faith. Jesus is the reason we fast—to be near him in a unique way that is contrary to our self-indulgent culture. And as we draw near to him, he draws near to us (Jas 4:8).

THE DISCIPLINE TO ENDURE

When I write about spiritual disciplines, I hesitate to give you many how-to instructions. That's because I was traumatized by heavy-handed advice on walking out my faith. I could tell you all the things you can do and perhaps should do, but if you do even one of those things because you feel it's your duty and not your delight, you won't continue in it. It's difficult to will ourselves to do something—even something that's good for us—if our only motivation is about us and not the Lord.

Think about diet plans. They are good for a season, but most don't last. And if you go on a quick-fix diet, you'll get exactly what you asked for—a quick fix—and then you'll return to your old self. We don't want to approach the Lord like a diet plan, a quick fix, or someone who can give us something for a moment. We need the Lord to sustain us for a lifetime, and he promises to do so. For you and me to endure in the disciplines, we need to ask the Lord to give us a heart that longs for him so we may run to him.

We don't practice spiritual disciplines because we think we'll earn God's favor for them. We practice them to help us finish well and to enjoy the Lord while we run the race. We discipline our bodies through prayer, Bible reading, fasting, solitude, and a host of other means, expressing our delight in and dependence on the Lord. That's how we work out our salvation in the fear of the Lord and build muscle that will last throughout the ages (Phil 2:12-13).

BROKEN AND CONTRITE

As I reflected on repentance and the need for it in my own life and in our culture, I quickly realized that in some Christian circles, people don't use the word *sin* much. I don't see it being written about often. Sometimes that word is avoided and replaced with other preferred words, like *brokenness* and *weakness*. Brokenness is absolutely part of the reality of who we are. We're broken people in need of grace and healing. But brokenness gives only part of the picture. Our brokenness could be a result of the harmful actions of others, but sin is different and much more specific.

As told in Genesis 3, sin came into the world, and everything changed.

Perhaps sin isn't something most of us think about. One of my closest friends never thought about her sin or the state of her heart (that is, whether or not she was struggling with sin). One area she struggled with was mild anxiety (neither clinical nor debilitating). She would use the words *anxious* and *worried* a lot, saying, "I'm really anxious about that test" or "I'm worried that my boyfriend no longer likes me." But she never considered that her anxiety could be related to sin. I'm not saying anxiety is always related to sin, but for her, the Lord in his kindness revealed that the anxiety she experienced at times was related to a lack of trust in God (see Mt 6:25-34; Phil 4:6; 1 Pet 5:6-7).

In 1 John 1:8 we read, "If we say we have no sin, we deceive ourselves, and the truth is not in us." My friend wasn't quite there. It was more likely that she was simply not convicted of her sin and not used to thinking in those categories. As she was discipled, she began to see her struggles for what they were. She was able to put a name on it and to experience freedom and peace. Like her, we need to see sin for what it is in order to fight it.

Wrapped as we are in broken, sinful bodies, we struggle and fall short in this life. Temptations that could be resisted defeat us at times. Strength and resolve fade, and our flesh continues to wage war against us for as long as we draw breath. Although at times we feel like quitting when we struggle and fail, it's critical that we don't. That we press on. That we turn in repentance from our sin and resume the race. When we've failed to be faithful to our Lord, we ask him for the grace to continue pressing on through prayer and reading his Word, knowing that we can do nothing apart from our Savior (Jn 15:5). Through it all, we're reminded that we are dependent on the love and grace of our Savior.

But let's face it—we mess up. We mess up daily. We mess up hourly. Yet our smallest offense deserves the full wrath of God. That's hard to hear if we forget that God has not only covered our sin in Christ but also allows us to approach him continually to receive that grace anew. We also know that God is holy—set apart in his perfection, glory, and majesty. We are sinners who sin every day.

As the Protestant reformer Martin Luther put it, we are *simul justus et peccator*, Latin for "simultaneous righteous and sinner." Although we're sinners and we battle with sin in our being every day, our Lord doesn't see us as such! Jesus' imputed righteousness covers our sin; he took our sin and transferred to us his righteousness. God looks at us and sees righteousness even as we fight against sin. Doesn't that grace make you want to fight against sin, to endure in the struggle, knowing that the sin is already forgiven?

THE FEAR OF GOD

Our sin should grieve us, but it cannot condemn us because we serve a God who is good and gracious but also holy and just. So, what are we to do with this enigma of our sinfulness and God's holiness that clings so close to us? Repent and receive God's amazing grace.

I used to be terrified of God. Yes. I said it. He reminded me of my childish imaginations of the boogeyman. I'd think, there he is again, that eerie dark shadow lurking in the closet. He seemed so unpredictable. What might he do next? What might happen? Will he jump out and get me? I fearfully snuggled into my bed, waiting for the boogeyman to jump out of the closet and get me.

When I became a Christian, I realized that I often related to God with that childlike fear of the boogeyman. I felt like I didn't have much control over my life. Instead of realizing I was in the hands of a good and loving Father, I viewed him as tyrannical. He had all the control, I thought, but the only love he showed was on the cross (which of course would have been enough).

Yes, I really did think God was like the boogeyman, just waiting for the right moment to punish me or cause some harm.

How sad. If we know God only as the sovereign ruler of the universe, it's unlikely we can trust him. Not until we understand the great love of God do we begin to see his ways as good and loving.

So, yes, those tough things in our lives come from God's loving hand (1 Pet 1:3-9; Heb 12:3-17). Yet we can rest in the knowledge that his thoughts are not our thoughts; his ways are not our ways; and he is ever mindful of us (Ps 8:4; Is 55:8).

We see evidence of this in Isaiah 55, which begins with an urgent call for us:

> Come, everyone who thirsts,
>   come to the waters;
> and he who has no money,
>   come, buy and eat!
> Come, buy wine and milk
>   without money and without price. (Is 55:1)

God delights in meeting our needs (spiritual and otherwise). We have a Father who invites us to the throne of grace to receive help (Heb 4:16). And though as a young Christian I didn't fully grasp the significance of the cross, I now understand that God displayed his ultimate love for us through the sacrifice of his Son on our behalf. Is there a greater love than that?

God is not the boogeyman. He is the sovereign, loving, awesome God who came to redeem a people for himself. He is good and loves us relentlessly. So in response to our knowledge of his loving character, we discipline ourselves to repent daily of the sin for which Christ has already died. Knowing this allows me to be honest when I fall short.

WALKING IN THE LIGHT

One of the many side effects I've experienced from getting older is an inability to see the road while driving at night. Everything glows. If it rains, it's as if someone is shining a bright light in my eyes. Like the responsible adult I am, I have yet to go to an eye doctor. So I'm driving around in the dark, blind as a bat.

Thankfully we don't have to do this as Christians. We've seen the light. The gospel has shined light into darkness. And this light isn't disorienting; it's a gift of grace that purifies and guides us.

But have you been walking around like you're still in the dark? God calls you to walk in the light. To walk in the light means to walk in the goodness and grace of God, living a life that is reflective of the Savior, and walking in a manner worthy of the gospel.

Repentance is one of the clearest ways to walk in this light. The apostle John tells us, "If we say we have fellowship with him while we walk in darkness, we lie and do not practice the truth" (1 Jn 1:6). To walk in darkness is either to walk with the knowledge of sin and ignore it or to walk as if we are completely without sin, never repenting (1 Jn 1:8). The grace of God allows us to not only acknowledge that we continue to struggle with sin, but also to turn from our sin.

We see clearly that walking in the light doesn't make us perfect—not even close. We will never reach perfection on this earth. That's why repentance is such a beautiful gift from our God. "If we confess our sins, he is faithful and just to forgive us our sins and to cleanse us from all unrighteousness" (1 Jn 1:9). What grace!

We confess our sins to God—acknowledging our great need for him to turn us from our sin—and what does he do? He does what he's already done—pouring out the grace we need to change. His wrath was reserved for Jesus. We don't receive punishment or wrath for our sins; we receive grace. There are, of course, consequences for sin, but even so, our standing before God doesn't change. God is sovereign and rules over all.

God is holy, yet because of Jesus we can approach him. "For our sake he made him to be sin who knew no sin, so that in him we might become the righteousness of God" (2 Cor 5:21). What amazing and unspeakable grace! Run, don't walk, to the throne of grace. Don't walk like a blind man while you can walk in the light that's available to you. Confess your sin and receive grace. There is no condemnation for you.

Headlights illuminate our way only so far as we drive. We can't see all that is ahead of us. The beams' short reach allows for a safe journey as we make our way down the road, and we need the light every mile of the way. As we journey and endure, we need the Lord to light our path and to help us shine the light into the darkness. He graciously gives us his Word to reveal his nature, his will, and his desire for us, which is truly the lamp for our feet and light for our path (Ps 119:105). We don't endure our repentance alone—God is with us, revealing our sin so we may be more and more like his Son. God wants to make good on his promise to finish the good work he began, and he will (Phil 1:6).

FINDING OUR WAY IN THE DARK

Today you might wonder if you've ever truly repented. If you think you haven't, ask the Lord for a broken and contrite heart. That kind of heart recognizes the wrong done against God and possibly others. It's an inner disposition that leads us to be able to say, "I have sinned, and against you only have I sinned." I have heard it said that when we confess, our sin is already forgiven. So ask God to make you aware of what you can confess. As King David wrote, "The sacrifices of God are a broken spirit; a broken and contrite heart, O God, you will not despise" (Ps 51:17).

And oh how I know the damage of resisting the call to humble myself. I remember a season in my relationship with a girlfriend when I was hurt deeply and allowed that hurt to transform into hatred. I hated her. I did. I can't sugarcoat it. But my grudge was hurting me. I struggled with being irritable when I encountered her in some way. I also battled fear that I might run into her. I was paranoid in my pride, afraid that she would slander me. It was a mess. It was sin. And the Lord was faithful to show me my unforgiveness and hate so I might repent, extend forgiveness and love to my neighbor, and enjoy life. It was so freeing!

I hate sin. It is ugly. It disrupts life. It messes with precious relationships. It confuses the mind. Sin is pervasive and gross. Sin affects us to our core. Sin wreaks havoc on much, but perhaps its greatest impact is on our ability to obey the commandments to love God with all our heart and soul and mind, and to love our neighbor as ourselves. Perhaps that's one reason Paul rebuked the Corinthians about their selfishness and division with verses all about love.

LEARNING FROM LOVE

In Paul's "love chapter" we read, "Love is patient and kind; love does not envy or boast; it is not arrogant or rude. It does not insist on its own way; it is not irritable or resentful; it does not rejoice in wrongdoing, but rejoices with the truth. Love bears all things, believes all things, hopes all things, endures all things" (1 Cor 13:4-7). Despite how familiar those verses may be, they truly are the way of love. The Corinthians had trouble loving one another. This revealed itself in various ways, but it came through most clearly in their pursuit of spiritual gifts. Some had elevated their gifts (or perhaps certain gifts) over others. Paul reminded them, "Now there are varieties of gifts, but the same Spirit; and there are varieties of service, but the same Lord" (1 Cor 12:4). He then spent considerable time explaining that the church has many parts but is one body (1 Cor 12:12-30). After all of that, Paul made it clear that we can use the gifts to elevate ourselves and thereby do so completely in vain—without true love for others and only for selfish gain and glory (1 Cor 13:1-3).

The correction to the Corinthians' selfishness is the same helpful correction to our selfishness and to the many sinful desires and struggles that cling so closely. If love is patient and kind, we can fight to learn to put on gentleness and kindness. Love doesn't insist on its own way—pride does—so we ask

God to give us humility. Love is not irritable or resentful; therefore every relationship should be doused in the patience and forbearance that can come only from the power of Christ. Love bears with others and is not selfish; love believes the truth and the best until proven otherwise. Love hopes for the absolute best in all situations and in the gospel that reconciles. Love endures with hardship and trouble.

Love doesn't give up.

Now, if you're like me after reading and reflecting on these commands to love, you're likely pleading with God for help. We don't love the way we ought. We fall short—woefully short. But God has given us his Spirit and his enabling, empowering grace. We don't love others because we're good people; we don't even love God because of anything in and of ourselves. "We love because he first loved us" (1 Jn 4:19). This is great news for us. It means we can ask God—the same God whose power changed our hearts of stone into hearts of flesh and whose power enables us to love him—to use the same power to enable us to love our neighbor as ourselves. We will fail, but there's repentance and forgiveness available. Let's call out to God for help to put off that nasty selfish sin—and to love.

African theologian Augustine of Hippo understood this broken and contrite heart that the Lord longs for us to experience. In his *Confessions*, he wrote, "'What shall I render to the Lord?' (Ps. 115:2) who recalls these things to my memory, but my soul feels no fear from the recollection. I will love you, Lord, and I will give thanks and confession to your name because you have forgiven me such great evils and my nefarious deeds."[1]

Truly understanding our sin and God's forgiveness of that sin shouldn't lead us to despair; rather, it should lead us to love and gratefulness. God has forgiven much. So there's something beautiful about the rawness of Augustine's writing and the simplicity of this particular proclamation: "I will love you, Lord, and I will give thanks."

Perhaps that's all we need to help us put off sin and enjoy the Lord. Maybe that's why God commands us to love him with all that is within us (Mt 22:37). As we love him, all other things fail to satisfy us—including our sin.

EXPERIENCING FREEDOM IN THE FIGHT

I used to have an incredibly weak conscience. When a sermon was preached, I was left feeling condemned, regardless of the content. If someone shared a correction in a small-group meeting, I figured out a way to apply it to my heart. I think this all started when I first learned about human depravity. I took the idea that we're sinful—dead and without hope apart from Jesus—to the extreme. I learned that everything we do is chock-full of sin, and I felt paralyzed as a result. I questioned if I could do anything good or without ill motives. This led me to mistrust everyone, as I thought, *If this is true, no one can be trusted.* And I walked in fear and despair for years.

Lacking in my understanding and perhaps in the teaching around me was the *imago Dei*. Yes, I was dead in my trespasses before I knew Jesus, but I was also created in the image of God before I accepted Jesus as my Lord and Savior. This means that there are indeed aspects of my nature and everyone else's that have the capability of reflecting our Lord and even bringing him glory prior to conversion. I believe that now wholeheartedly.

Although I also wholeheartedly believe we can do nothing apart from our Lord, I do think that we can unconsciously do things that reflect him. We don't have to acknowledge that our delight in a sunset is because of our Creator God, but as we delight—just as he delights—we are a reflection of him.

When we look at someone and see beauty, is it because that person is created by God? I think so. If we can see people's humanness and delight in them, it isn't because they are *just* people. They carry the *imago Dei*.

And why do we laugh? Because we reflect our merciful, beautiful, joyful God. Why do we long to serve and care for the poor? Why do we see someone fall and then bend over to help her back up? We don't pause and think, *I should pick her up, but if I do, I wonder if she'll think I'm only doing it to bring attention to myself.* That level of self-examination is oppressive.

Nothing we do is perfect; only Jesus is perfect (1 Pet 2:22). But we don't need to walk around afraid that we're sinning. What freedom is that? If Christ set us free, then we are free indeed (Jn 8:36). But if we're constantly aware of our sin, then we aren't truly free. To be clear, I'm not swinging in the opposite direction and saying that we don't need to be aware of sin at all. The apostle Paul helps us understand this: "What shall we say then? Are we to continue in sin that grace may abound? By no means! How can we who died to sin still live in it?" (Rom 6:1-2). No, we don't desire to go on sinning so that grace may increase. We are told to confess our sins (1 Jn 1:9). And God's kindness leads to repentance (Rom 2:4). Yes, it's his kindness.

Here's another aspect of my weak conscience that was revealed: I had a constant need to ask others for forgiveness. I felt that if I asked, the guilt would be washed away, so I could move forward. Of course, this was pride masked as humility. We don't need to repent to feel better about ourselves or to feel that we can *now* approach the Lord. We repent because God is kind to show us more of himself—and more of him means less of us. More of him is sanctification, being made into Jesus' likeness from one degree of glory to the next (2 Cor 3:18). We do repent out of guilt, but it's not the oppressive guilt that so many of us place on ourselves.

I don't want to grieve the Spirit with my sin, but I wonder if all of my heart examination in the past was just as grievous. I was saying to the Lord that what Jesus did on the cross wasn't enough. Sure, I was no longer condemned for the wrongs I'd done in the past, but deep down, I struggled to believe that Jesus' sacrifice could cover my present sins. And though there are Scriptures about doing good, loving others, serving with a glad heart, etc., there's no way I could do any of that on my own. But here's the thing about our awesome and good God: he isn't going to command us to do something without giving us the grace and strength to do it. And because he knew we'd never be able to do everything he commanded us, he sent his Son Jesus to be the perfect (*perfect!*) substitute.

MOVING FORWARD IMPERFECTLY

The past several years have brought renewal for me. I now understand that I'm imperfectly moving forward but there's grace present and grace available for you and for me. There's grace to serve with pure motives. There's grace to love without wanting something in return. There's grace to have joy and not to feel guilty because there's destruction all around. There's grace for living and setting our eyes on Jesus and his goodness and not our own (or lack thereof).

If you've been paralyzed by your awareness of sin in your life, remember the gospel. The gospel isn't just for our conversion; it's for our daily living. Remember it all—not just that he died for your sins but also that he rose, conquering death. Remember that the accuser wants you to be paralyzed by your sin so you aren't effective for the kingdom. Jesus really is better. Remember that he has cast your sin from you "as far as the east is from the west" (Ps 103:12).

DON'T GO IT ALONE

Love bears all things, believes all things,
hopes all things, endures all things.

1 Corinthians 13:7

This race we've been given to run isn't a call to a solo effort. We are to function in community, encouraging, supporting, challenging, and building one another up. We are a team. If we go it alone, we go against the way God designed us to live. We need help along the way, and we need to be an encouragement and support to others as well. But sometimes community is hard and may make it hard for us to endure.

I told an old pastor that if I just lived a certain way on the outside, conforming my behavior to the accepted Christian norms of that local church, no one within the church would ever ask me about my walk with God. They would assume—from what they observed—that I was walking in faithful obedience to God.

The external practices shared by the members in my church were all good things. The problem came when, at a certain point, some of the members twisted the gospel, equating some specific practices with godliness and placing matters of personal preference on the same level as the Word of God.

Maybe you've experienced this in your context as well. Some elevate things like small-group attendance while others elevate schooling preferences for your children. It doesn't seem to matter what's going on in the hearts of those who live a certain way; they are automatically considered godly as long as they follow the accepted practices.

This was a difficult season for me as I was trying to discern what's true godliness and what's fueled by culture and legalism. I struggled to understand grace. I struggled to understand the gospel. And I struggled to know what is true and what is just opinion. I wasn't sure if I'd ever love the church again. I wasn't sure if I even wanted to attend church. But there was something—Someone—greater pulling me toward that glorious and broken institution.

In Ephesians 5:22-33 are specific instructions for how husbands and wives relate to one another. At the same time, Paul also gave us a beautiful picture of the gospel and how Christian marriage reflects the relationship between Christ and his church.

> Wives, submit to your own husbands, as to the Lord. For the husband is the head of the wife even as Christ is the head of the church, his body, and is himself its Savior. Now as the church submits to Christ, so also wives should submit in everything to their husbands.
>
> Husbands, love your wives, as Christ loved the church and gave himself up for her, that he might sanctify her, having cleansed her by the washing of water with the

word, so that he might present the church to himself in splendor, without spot or wrinkle or any such thing, that she might be holy and without blemish. In the same way husbands should love their wives as their own bodies. He who loves his wife loves himself. For no one ever hated his own flesh, but nourishes and cherishes it, just as Christ does the church, because we are members of his body. "Therefore a man shall leave his father and mother and hold fast to his wife, and the two shall become one flesh." This mystery is profound, and I am saying that it refers to Christ and the church. However, let each one of you love his wife as himself, and let the wife see that she respects her husband. (Eph 5:22-33)

We are prone to focusing only on the commands given to wives and husbands in this passage. But don't miss all that God is saying about what Jesus accomplished through the cross. In Ephesians 5, we get a glimpse into the marital love that Jesus has for his bride, the church. The church isn't a pragmatic way to organize Christians for maximum effectiveness—it's far more. The church is the object of Jesus' intense focus and love. Here are ways the New Testament speaks about Jesus' love for the church:

- Christ is the head of the church. He is the reason the church exists. Without Christ, there is no church (Col 1:18).

- Jesus is the Savior of the church. His death made a way for people to approach God, and we are now counted as brothers and sisters in Christ (Eph 3:12; Rom 12:5).

- Christ loved the church and gave himself up for her (Rom 5:8). This is God's amazing demonstration of love for us.

- Jesus sanctifies and cleanses his bride, the church (1 Jn 1:9; Phil 1:6).

- Jesus stands in our place, intercedes for us, and will one day present his bride as spotless like him (Rom 8:34; 1 Cor 1:30; 1 Jn 3:2).

- Christ doesn't hate his body; he nourishes it (Eph 5:29).

When you read these truths and realize they apply to you, doesn't it make your heart sing? It's amazing how much Jesus loves his people. And we know that these truths aren't in reference to just one individual but to the church as a whole—that is, all people who have trusted in Jesus for their salvation. If Jesus loves the church this much, there's no doubt that we ought to love it as well.

Understanding all that Jesus has done motivates me to press in to love and serve the body. He was sinned against, so we will be as well. The difference is, Jesus never sinned. We, however, will sin against others and need the grace that Jesus has provided.

I've been a member of only a few different local churches since I became a Christian. Those churches came with their unique joys and sorrows. But I know I need the church, and the church needs me. We aren't called to walk out our faith alone. Paul gave us a picture of our mutual need for one another in 1 Corinthians 12:12-26: the church is one body with many parts, each part having an important role to play. If we are to run the race, we need not only legs and feet but also a heart and lungs and eyes and ears and a circulatory system and a digestive system. We need every part to finish the race set before us.

But if we allow hurts and sin to divide the body, it simply won't function as it should. Because of sin, the church will always be a slightly dysfunctional family, but we can continually grow in love for one another. This kind of growth is possible only when we set our eyes on the cross of Christ and our resurrected King. Jesus' sacrifice enables us to love the broken church and to contribute to her, knowing that one day he will come back for his bride, and we will worship perfectly as one.[1]

THE BEAUTY OF THE CHURCH

You and I need a vision for the importance and beauty of the church and the need for her to persevere through the tough times brought on by our sin. As we get this vision for the beauty of the church, even in the midst of all its brokenness, it isn't enough to simply agree that "church" is a biblical concept. Church is a people we live with. Church is a family—the family of God (Eph 2:19-22). If you're truly in community, sharing each other's lives, being open about sin, meeting together, and encouraging one another, then there will be a time when you wrong one another.

We are not isolated individuals; we have a family history. Some people can trace their ancestors back for centuries. Similarly we've inherited the faith from centuries of faithful forefathers and foremothers who went before us. And that communion of saints extends across space and time to enable us to run the race into the future. Jesus said that the gates of hell will not prevail against the church (Mt 16:18). His heart for his church reminds me that this family of God we are a part of is worth fighting for even when the strain of relationships and sorrows in the church seem too much to bear.

You've likely heard the saying, church is not a building. But living out this reality takes us far beyond slogans and platitudes. To say we are a family is also nothing new. For some, going to church is easy, but building relationships is hard. But because we need each other and because sometimes life is confusing and includes insurmountable circumstances, it's important to press into the life of the church beyond attending once a week. Actually it's essential to the faith God has called us to. Just as we need a theological vision for the church, we need a similar vision for the outworking of life in the church. We need something God's Word addresses: discipleship.

Discipleship can take many forms. It can be as simple as inviting someone into your kitchen for fellowship to organizing a routine lunch. However it looks, it involves honesty, seeking advice, Scripture, and someone willing to do all of the above. The body of Christ doesn't exist for us to gather on Sundays and then move along with our lives. God's Word paints a picture of believers being a part of each other's lives (Acts 2:44-47).

Seeking counsel and being discipled are two ways to invite others into your life. People won't know the details of your life unless you're willing to share them. A willingness to be discipled by another provides an opportunity for prayer and mutual encouragement. We pursue one another "because we are members of his body" (Eph 5:30). The Preacher in Ecclesiastes wrote, "Two are better than one, because they have a good reward for their toil. For if they fall, one will lift up his fellow. But woe to him who is alone when he falls and has not another to lift him up!" (Eccles 4:9-10). He's writing about the vanity of trying to work alone to outdo others.

Getting things done isn't the only benefit of working together. Two are better than one as we live out our faith in Christ. We truly need each other, though we often try to go it alone. We need reproof and instruction, though we seldom seek it. This is why discipleship is so important.

Our temptation may be to think we know what's best for ourselves. As you've heard—and maybe said—before, "We know ourselves better than anyone."

Scripture says that we may be more confused than we think. The heart is deceitful, so to trust yourself at all times is not the best route to take (Jer 17:9). Wise counsel from a friend, pastor, or someone in your community group could be just the thing God uses for your protection.

One proverb says that a wise man will hear and learn, and will acquire wise counsel (Prov 1:5). So we can safely assume that an unwise man will not hear from others; he will shut them down and not listen. He will lack understanding and will not acquire wise counsel. So we need to resist the temptation to be wise in our own eyes (Prov 3:7), which isn't easy! As we seek to gain understanding, we must first acknowledge that we don't always know what's best.

Paul wrote that the older women in the church should teach what is good and train the younger women (Titus 2:3). They were to equip other women in how to walk in step with the truth of the gospel. And this isn't a suggestion—it is God's instruction for how we should relate to one another. This is Discipleship 101, yet another proof that we need each other. We can't obey the commands in Titus 2 without being willing to be discipled (and being available and willing to disciple others).[2]

I became a Christian as an adult. One of the first things the Lord did upon my salvation was illuminate his Word to me regarding the family of God. Those first precious years of my new Christian faith would have been strained without the friendships and consistent fellowship of those around me in my local church. The Lord specifically brought a white woman from Chicago and a first-generation Chinese woman from Nashville. (I share their ethnicities because this was an answer to prayer for me. I had longed for diverse friends, and the Lord gave me them right away.) We met every other week to share each other's lives, confess sin, pray for one another, and laugh a lot. It was a gift.

When I first became a Christian, I was beyond excited about Jesus, but as in a marriage, the relationship only began at the wedding. There would be a lifetime of learning and growing together.

I knew I needed others to help me along, and so do you. Consistent accountability to others in my church has been a means of God's protection. To this day, though I'm further along in my walk than I was a decade ago, I still know I'm capable of sin (1 Cor 10:12). I am a new creation, and I have the Spirit's power, but it's no longer a surprise that when I want to do good, "evil lies close at hand" (Rom 7:21). Understanding that we're all batting on the same team (all have sinned) means we can freely share with close, trusted friends. Accountability allows us to confess patterns of temptation. In so doing, we are restrained from actual transgression.

The point behind relationships in the church isn't just to share about sin and to hear hard words of rebuke. Though the wounds of a friend are a sign of his faithfulness (Prov 27:6), fellowship and building relationships in the church should also be a time to build each other up and to encourage each other toward God's goodness and grace found on the cross of Christ. We can't read and apply much of the New Testament without the church body. The church allows us to apply the "one another" verses found in the Scriptures. My friends and I reminded each other who we were in Christ: accepted completely, daughters of the Most High, and forgiven. We reminded each other that we knew Jesus—he is ours and we are his—and we could draw near to him and his throne of grace.

In community with one another we have the opportunity to express genuine love because God has transformed our friends into siblings. We are brothers and sister in Christ; as such we are to be devoted to one another (Jn 15:17; Rom 12:10). We have those opportunities only if we don't neglect meeting together (Heb 10:25). Life in Christ takes effort and commitment and sacrifice. In the end we'll be thankful for it.

Ultimately, true relationships in the church can be a means by which God draws us to himself. Self-sufficiency says we don't need anyone, but humility shouts for help from those God has placed in our lives. This habit of sharing and praying with others will inevitably teach us how to cast our cares on the only One who can fully bear their weight and who loves us with an unfailing love (1 Pet 5:7). God graciously reminds us that apart from him we can do nothing. And a great means of that reminder are the brothers and sisters he puts in our lives.[3]

Don't go it alone. You were made for community, and you are needed in your community. If you don't have one, pray the Lord would give you a church you can call home. The Christian walk is hard enough; intentionally doing it on your own is not his plan for you. I know that sounds strong and direct. That's because as messed up as the church can be, it's exactly the reason Jesus came and died. He died for messed-up people like you and me, and he calls all of us messed-up people to come together to proclaim unity and peace to a broken world. As Natasha Robinson shares in her book *A Sojourner's Truth*, "We are all broken, imperfect people called to serve broken, imperfect people."[4]

That's radical. And it's true.

WE ARE NEVER ALONE

Most miscarriages have few to no symptoms, but mine was full of them. Early in pregnancy, things felt off, and I became easily winded and dizzy. A few days after a worried call to my nurse, the bleeding came. I was home, by myself, and in excruciating pain.

When I became pregnant the first time, my husband and I assumed a baby would come nine months later. Miscarriage never crossed our minds. Many of my friends were having babies, and it all looked so easy. So my loss was a lonely one.

People said all types of things to encourage me: *You'll get pregnant again. You'll get to hold your baby in heaven. At least it was early on in the pregnancy.* We had announced our pregnancy immediately, so I also had people ask about the baby months after the miscarriage. It felt like a never-ending reminder of our loss.

And then it happened again.

A few months after the first miscarriage, thinking the chances of a second miscarriage were slim, we had begun trying for another. We were thrilled when I became pregnant again; we saw this baby as an answer to our prayers. During this pregnancy, I'd feel something and wonder about a potential miscarriage, but mostly I was just happy to be pregnant again. Then we had a routine ultrasound, and there was no heartbeat. The miscarriage came with complications. My body didn't respond well to the medicine, leaving me with a chronic stomach condition.

After my second miscarriage, fear and confusion reigned in my mind and heart. How could I make sense of a sovereign and good God in the midst of it? Why could my friend who didn't want children have them so easily, but I couldn't? I was bitter—and finished. I asked my husband if we could take a break from any attempt at getting pregnant so that my heart, mind, and body could heal.

The Lord revealed to me that my mixture of isolation, fear, and despondency wasn't an anomaly. Jesus was denied and abandoned by his friends. He pleaded in the garden for the Lord to take the cup away and then proceeded down the awful lonely road toward the cross. And how could we forget the cry of our Savior as he died on the cross: "'Eli, Eli, lema sabach-thani?' that is, 'My God, my God, why have you forsaken me?'" (Mt 27:46).

God provided comfort through the suffering of his Son. I wasn't alone in my pain. And he began to reveal to me that he understood and he loved me dearly. I didn't have any-where else to go but to him, and he had answered my cry in the wilderness. It was comforting to realize that it was okay to be in a wilderness. Jesus didn't go to the cross cheering and clapping. He was sorrowful—sorrowful for this world and for the pain and separation from his Father he knew he'd have to endure. So it was okay for me to weep. Through my tears, I found great hope because I knew I wasn't praying to a dead savior. He had risen and was indeed interceding on my behalf.

The church also began to rally around me in ways I had never experienced (or expected!). Friends visited. People texted me to give me Scripture verses or just to let me know they were thinking of me. And then there was the food—yes, food. A group of servant friends cooked meals for us. (We experienced this generosity again when we finally had our firstborn two years later.)

Then I was terrified to find out I was pregnant again. Every strange feeling in my abdomen set off a series of imaginary scenarios in my mind, each ending with me in the hospital then coming home without a child. We waited a little longer to tell friends, but we soon wanted everyone we knew to pray for us. We knew we couldn't handle the pain and suffering of an-other miscarriage alone.

Along with learning that the Lord endured great suffering, I realized that many other women had experienced miscarriages but hadn't spoken of them. They began to comfort me with the comfort they had received from the Lord.

God used the church to help meet both our physical needs and our spiritual ones. We didn't have to endure alone. We couldn't have.[5]

FALLING AND GETTING UP

For the righteous falls seven times and rises again,
but the wicked stumble in times of calamity.

PROVERBS 24:16

King David is one of the most well-known figures in the Bible, besides Paul and Jesus himself. In his youth he fought the giant Goliath. He's also known for his patience with King Saul and his friendship with Jonathan. We get the term "a man after God's own heart" because it's the way God described David (Acts 13:22). He was a man to be admired and imitated. He was a man of great integrity—until he wasn't.

Just as David is popular for the good he did, he's also known for his great fall. He coveted another man's wife and took her as his own (2 Sam 11:2-4). He not only sinned against her; he defiled her, lied about it, and eventually had her husband killed (2 Sam 11:12-13; 12:9). David broke much of God's law during this fall into sin. He coveted, lied, committed adultery, and murdered.[1] How does anyone survive such a fall from grace?

One of the wonderful aspects of this story is Nathan. Nathan was a good friend to David, a true friend. He was sent by God to rebuke David by first appealing to his conscious through a parable of a different injustice (2 Sam 12:1-5). As soon as David became indignant about the man in Nathan's story, Nathan proclaimed, "You are the man!" (2 Sam 12:7). Nathan then told him the Lord's charge against him.

This scene reminds me of Jesus talking with the Samaritan woman, who proclaimed to the people after they met, "Come, see a man who told me all that I ever did" (Jn 4: 29). We can't hide our sin from God. He knows all and sees all. David had forgotten that God knew what he had done. It can be tempting to hide our sin, but it's just as bad to be blind to our sin. David knew he had done something wrong; otherwise he wouldn't have lied about it. But it took Nathan telling him everything he had done for David to see clearly and repent.

RECEIVING FORGIVENESS

In God's kindness to us, we not only get to read the story of David's fall, we also get to see the richness of his sorrow over it. Psalm 51 was written after Nathan's rebuke of David, who was not only a king but also a psalmist who wrote many of the psalms we read today.

Psalm 51 is not only insightful, it's also instructive. David cried out to the Lord for mercy by appealing to God's own character:

Have mercy on me, O God,
according to your steadfast love;
according to your abundant mercy. (Ps 51:1)

He pleaded to be washed clean of his transgressions. And he recognized that his sin, though committed against other people, was ultimately against God (Ps 51:4). As I read through this psalm, I can almost feel the agony and deep desire for forgiveness. David was broken, even to the point of saying that his bones were broken. That's how deep his sorrows went—to his bones.

God did forgive David of his sin (2 Sam 12:13), which is remarkable and even astounding. God could have struck him dead. God could have held his sin against him for good. God was instead true to his character: he was merciful. Although God forgave, the consequences of David's sins remained. The Lord said, "Because by this deed you have utterly scorned the Lord, the child that is born to you shall die" (2 Sam 12:14). Yet after all of this, we still see that David worshiped the Lord (2 Sam 12:20).

We can learn a great deal from David's story. When I read about him, I see how he focused on repentance. But let's consider how he finished his race. As we've seen in these passages, David did what may be considered unforgiveable in today's culture. We put people to death for committing murder and put them in prison for a lifetime for being an accomplice to murder. Sin does deserve punishment, and it is right to want to exercise justice against crimes. This may be why David receiving such forgiveness seems irrational and amazing. But can a man or woman recover from something so devastating? Is it possible to live a life that glorifies the Lord after such shameful behavior?

The rest of David's life was difficult, though he had suffered much. Yet he never stopped worshiping the Lord.

It's easy to read about these situations in the Scriptures and detach them from our own lives. It's easier to rejoice that David was forgiven than for us to experience a friend receiving mercy for adultery. I'll never forget the day one of my dearest friends experienced her husband's betrayal. The rage I felt was overwhelming. I wanted to do physical harm to him on my friend's behalf. I was angry and self-righteous. *How could God forgive such a man?* I thought. Aren't we glad that God isn't like us?!

What we also must see is that if we mess up big-time, that doesn't have to be the end of our story. There may be a lifetime of consequences, but that doesn't mean that on our deathbed we can't proclaim Jesus. It doesn't mean that we won't hear the words "Well done." If the Christian walk is about never sinning, none of us would hear those two words.

To be clear, this grace is not an excuse to sin. God knows our hearts, and as Paul wrote, we are not to sin deliberately so grace may increase (Rom 6:1). On the contrary, we work hard to finish the race, submitting our whole selves to the Lord. Many will fall. What you need to know is that you can get back up.

ARE YOU A BRUISED REED?

I wonder if David could be considered a bruised reed. He was an abuser, adulterer, and murderer—that we know for sure. But he was also a mighty man equated with strength. And his outer shell and inner pride needed refinement. He was bruised, battered, and fragile once his sin was revealed. I do wonder if it was a relief for him. No more pretending. No more hiding. Now all of him was laid bare and out in the open. He could accept being broken, and that was a gift.

The idea of a bruised reed comes from the prophet Isaiah as he prophesied about Jesus:

Behold my servant, whom I uphold,
  my chosen, in whom my soul delights;
I have put my Spirit upon him;
  he will bring forth justice to the nations.
He will not cry aloud or lift up his voice,
  or make it heard in the street;
a bruised reed he will not break,
  and a faintly burning wick he will not quench;
  he will faithfully bring forth justice. (Is 42:1-3)

There's an interesting contrast here. In its context, Isaiah is comparing the powerful nation of Israel and wicked rulers to the meekness of the Messiah (Is 41:2, 25). But we also see a beautiful contrast in Jesus. He is strong and will bring about justice in all the earth, yet he is merciful and will not break a bruised reed. This is a contrast but not a contradiction. In his goodness and grace, he brings about justice, and in his goodness and grace, he is merciful to the weak.

A bruised reed could mean several things, including a person who has been abused or mistreated. That person would be like a flimsy, thin plant, about to break at any moment. A bruised reed is someone who is weak in some way, as we see in Matthew 12:9-21. Jesus healed a man with a weak hand and then Matthew referenced Isaiah 42. In any case, a bruised reed is someone who has been humbled and is contrite in spirit (Is 57:15).

There's another character in the Scriptures who was strong on the outside but eventually crumbled: Peter.

We may be familiar with Peter's denial of Jesus, but it's the details of the event that cause me to take heed lest I fall

(1 Cor 10:12). In Luke 22:31-34, we see that Jesus not only knew Peter would deny him, he also prayed that Peter would be strengthened to serve more fervently after the denial. As Jesus headed to his death, he prayed for his friend's faltering faith even as he knew it would falter. He also prayed that when Peter repented, he would be used to strengthen his brothers. Jesus knew Peter would fail, and he knew that, because of God's undaunted mercy, failure would be a catalyst that would make Peter a leader of the church.

Peter, however, was confident in his own strength. No way would he deny Jesus, he thought. No way would he abandon his friend. Here is the scene:

> [Jesus said,] "Simon, Simon, behold, Satan demanded to have you, that he might sift you like wheat, but I have prayed for you that your faith may not fail. And when you have turned again, strengthen your brothers." Peter said to him, "Lord, I am ready to go with you both to prison and to death." Jesus said, "I tell you, Peter, the rooster will not crow this day, until you deny three times that you know me." (Lk 22:31-34)

As we see in this text, Peter thought he was ready to go to prison for Jesus. He was strong. He also was appalled that his Savior and friend could think he'd be a betrayer.

But we know the story: Peter denied Jesus, not once, not twice, but three times (Lk 22:54-62). The one disciple who had stood by Jesus kept his distance when it mattered most. He said he didn't know him. He said he wasn't one of the Twelve. Peter lied. He failed. He rejected God. But in sweet mercy, Peter turned.

Failure wasn't the end of Peter's story. He didn't deny Jesus and then move on; he wept. He knew he had sinned. He knew he had done just what Jesus said he would, even though he had stubbornly refused to believe it was possible. He was ashamed and broken because of his sin, which is mercy in itself.

If you read through the book of Acts, you'll quickly see that Peter was a changed man. Far from being fearful, he stood as a bold servant who proclaimed the gospel in the face of opposition. That is the power of God's mercy.

David and Peter could both be considered bruised reeds. Their sins were revealed, and they were shown to be broken and weak. We see this especially as we read the psalms of David. What a shame it would have been had these men never come to that point of brokenness, vulnerability, and repentance.

BRUISED BUT NOT DEFEATED

Here's what we need to remind our hearts of every day, especially if we fall into grave sin: Jesus will not break us. Let this truth guide you toward his grace to repent. Let this truth allow you to face today with confidence, not in your flesh but in your Savior.

Jesus is not out to get us. There are consequences for our sin, but if we have placed our faith in the finished work of Jesus Christ, wrath will not be poured out on us. Don't wait to humble yourself before him. You can confess your sin and turn right now. We don't have to wait for God to humble us; we can humble ourselves in his sight. David and Peter deserved to be bruised and crushed for their sin, but God poured out mercy. He will do the same for you.

You? Yes, you. I want you to believe this truth more than anything else. More importantly God wants us to know this truth, and he graciously put it in his Word: "He who did not spare his own Son but gave him up for us all, how will he not also with him graciously give us all things?" (Rom 8:32). In Romans, we are told that God is for us, and if God is for us, no one can be against us. We don't have to fear God's judgment and wrath because of our sin. God spared his own son; why would he then withhold forgiveness of the sins he died for? Condemnation is absolutely ridiculous in light of the sacrifice of Jesus. Though it's sometimes hard to believe that God forgives, he does and he will. He invites you and me to confess, and he'll do the rest—washing away the sin and shame.

AMAZING GRACE

John Newton was an eighteenth-century pastor and writer most famous for the beautifully written and often-sung hymn "Amazing Grace." But in his early life, Newton was an unrepentant slave trader. He'd had a tumultuous upbringing, losing his mother at a young age and bouncing around from ship to ship with his father. After a series of rough circumstances, including being homeless and begging for food, Newton found work on slave ships.

In 1747 a deadly situation turned into a mercy. While sailing, Newton's ship encountered a ferocious storm. Although Newton wasn't a Christian, he had been reading works by Christians and reading God's Word. Through the storm, the Lord drew Newton to himself.

Newton continued to work on slave ships for a while, though he tried to treat the slaves with dignity. He would soon realize that wasn't enough.

After nine years in the slave trade, Newton began work as a minister and soon joined forces with men like William Wilberforce in campaigning to end the slave trade altogether. In 1747, Newton wrote "Thoughts upon the African Slave Trade," in which he expresses his disgust in himself and for the business: "I hope it will always be a subject of humiliating reflection to me, that I was, once, an active instrument, in the business at which my heart now shudders."[2]

Newton could be considered a bruised reed—broken and contrite before the Lord and eager to right the wrongs of his many years of oppressing people made in the image of God.

In 1779, nearly ten years before he wrote the manifesto against slavery, he wrote the hymn "Amazing Grace." Perhaps these lyrics had a double meaning:

Amazing grace! how sweet the sound
That saved a wretch; like me!
I once was lost, but now am found,
Was blind, but now I see.[3]

He was lost and without God, but by the mercy and amazing grace of our Lord, Newton was given sight—salvation. God who saves to the uttermost also lifted his blindness toward slavery to see it for what it was. He was a wretched man, but the Lord saved him and used him for great good to benefit the church and the African people.

LOOKING TO THE PRIZE

The man who expects soon to remove will have his mind much taken up with the country to which he is going.

LEMUEL HAYNES

Before we know it, we will see our king. The dying person knows this well. My friend shared with me that as she sat beside her young dying husband, he said he wanted her to keep living and to enjoy life because he would be fine. He was going to meet their Maker. Holocaust survivor Corrie ten Boom related to this sentiment and wrote: "You can never learn that Christ is all you need, until Christ is all you have."[1]

In this last chapter, I hope you and I can gaze upon the beauty of the Lord and fix our eyes on the country to come. Even if we haven't yet learned that Christ is all we need, we can prepare our hearts and minds now for the realization that he is truly all we have. He is the only sure thing, the only lasting one. He is everlasting, as is his love.

LOOKING TO THE COUNTRY TO COME

We've already looked at Paul's analogy of an athlete who disciplines his body and how we ought to discipline our bodies for the Lord, namely in exercising self-control (1 Cor 9:24-25). But what he says in verse 26 is of utmost importance to us as we endure the race set before us: "So I do not run aimlessly; I do not box as one beating the air." There is a goal, there is a reason, and there is direction in our race. Like athletes, we look toward a finish line and a reward. Every step matters. If we don't remind ourselves that there's a purpose to our running, we won't finish well.

Paul reminded himself. He lived a life of suffering, so his encouragement to us carries weight and validity. He was tested in ways many of us will never have to endure. James also tells us that we are blessed by our enduring: "Blessed is the man who remains steadfast under trial, for when he has stood the test he will receive the crown of life, which God has promised to those who love him" (Jas 1:12). The crown of life resembles the wreath awarded to an athlete after a race—the same reward mentioned in 1 Corinthians 9:25 above.

By now it's clear that while there's enjoyment to be had in walking worthy of our calling, it's also quite hard. And so a reminder of the prize we are working toward is important.

But some people struggle with a focus on rewards in heaven. To them it seems like a selfish motivation for running the race set before us. But surely God wouldn't have told us that we receive a reward if he didn't also want us to look forward to that reward. Rewards are the proof that our labor and steadfastness are not in vain (1 Cor 15:58).

So, what is this reward we look forward to?

In this life, we are being made more like Christ. One day, we will be face to face with our Savior. And so we press on toward the goal to win the prize. One prize, and likely the greatest, is being in perfect fellowship with Jesus forever (Phil 3:14).

Our treasures will last forever; they will never rot or be destroyed (Lk 12:33-34). We will have no more sin. We will be glorified—made absolutely perfect (Rom 8:30). There will be no more suffering or pain (Rev 21:4), no more enduring. There will be no need for this book or books like it. Praise God! There will be perfect peace.

As we resolve and persevere now, the Holy Spirit transforms and refines our will, desires, and joys. On that day when we are with our Lord and Savior, it won't be because of what we've done but because of his work on our behalf. It will be our great joy—then, as well as today—to honor and glorify him with all we have.

I don't know about you, but this is almost more than I can handle. I can't wait! When I know a vacation is coming shortly, I attempt to get as much accomplished in my home as humanly possible because I don't enjoy coming home from vacation to a disorganized and dirty house. When we know summer is coming, our workouts and exercise increase. When we're about to move into a new home, it's best not to wait to the last minute to think through the details and pack (although I know you might).

We Christians have something to look forward to, something we should feel great eagerness for. We are anticipating a time when all sorrows will be wiped away. We are anticipating a time when the kingdom will be consummated. We are anticipating the unity of all tribes, tongues, and nations. Can you imagine that? In our divided world, it's hard to imagine, but it's what we anticipate (Rev 7:9-11). We are anticipating being with the Lord forever. In remembering that this earth is not our home, that we truly do have a citizenship in heaven, we instruct our hearts and minds as we interact with the world around us and persevere to the end.

WAITING WELL

So we wait. And we wait with anticipation.

The apostle Paul waited well, and inspired by the Holy Spirit, he gives us a vision for how we too can wait well. His story is told and retold, and for good reason. Early in his life, he terrorized the church. He described himself as a Hebrew of Hebrews, Pharisee, persecutor of the church, and blameless according to the law (Phil 3:1-6). His conversion took away his worldly status among the Jews, and he counted it all as loss because of the surpassing worth of knowing Christ (Phil 3:7). He suffered, was imprisoned, and even was slandered in the church. But it was all nothing compared to gaining Christ.

Fixing our eyes on eternity helps us to fight for joy. If we don't lose heart, we can enjoy today because the Lord is at hand; it is the day that he has made. We know that there's a perfect eternity to look forward to and that the troubles of today won't have the last word (2 Cor 4:16-18). While all of this is true, we can still marvel at what God has done here, knowing that in time he will make all things new. Eternity has everything to do with our enjoyment today.

Today we get glimpses of heaven, tastes of the everlasting joy that we will experience. Think of the things you enjoy; the Lord has enabled such joy and has given those good gifts (Jas 1:17). From a delicious meal that is a foretaste of how we will feast in heaven to moments when you never want worship to end—something we will get to experience soon enough—these glimpses of heaven are God's kindness to us and can help us endure. He's given us good things.

Even with the security of knowing that our future contains everlasting peace and joy, it's difficult to wait and maintain an eternal perspective. Regardless of our situation in life—rich or poor, young or old—it can be difficult to fix our eyes on what is yet to be seen. We can practice the following four ways to daily fix our eyes on eternity with anticipation, which will impact the way we live today.

1. Preach the gospel to yourself. I've heard this over the years, and it has stuck with me. Preaching the gospel to yourself is doing exactly as it sounds. In doing that, we remind ourselves of the truth found in the gospel. We need to remind ourselves that there is a real battle we fight with sin, and there is great forgiveness in Christ. We need to remember there is no condemnation for those who are in Christ Jesus. And we need to remember that Jesus is the risen King and is interceding for us. All that Jesus has accomplished in the gospel frees us to enjoy God's good gifts. When we forget the truth of the gospel—that all good things come from the Father—we often find ourselves mired in guilt, condemnation, legalism, and idolatry, which keep us from enjoying life today as we wait for our future glory.

2. Fight idolatry. Idolatry can be tough to pinpoint until something happens to the thing we value most or the thing we've placed our hope in. For some, work is such an idol that it not only hinders the enjoyment of rest, it also becomes difficult for us to enjoy the blessing of work. For others, hope is found in relationships, which means if something negative affects the relationship, it leads to despair, anger, or strife. Any time we begin to worship the created thing rather than the Creator, we lose sight of what's eternal, of what matters most. Everything on this earth is wasting away and not worthy of our worship. Only God is worthy of our worship. God alone will always provide perfect joy, peace, and love.

Until our faith becomes sight, we need to fight the temptation to forget our Savior and to turn to the worship of far lesser things. God tells us to have no other god before him. When we go against this command, it only takes away our true joy.

3. Remember time. We deal in twenty-four-hour cycles. We wake up, work, play, eat, go to bed, and do it all over again. The concept of eternity requires imagination; it's almost unfathomable and most definitely mysterious. However, life is hard, and although our experience of time reveals that everything has a beginning and an end, life can feel like an eternity. God's Word brings comfort and clarity as we wait. As Paul wrote, "For this light momentary affliction is preparing for us an eternal weight of glory beyond all comparison, as we look not to the things that are seen but to the things that are unseen" (2 Cor 4:17-18). The trials of life, the burdens of today, and the twenty-four-hour cycles that seem to be on endless repeat are only momentary. Every hour and every affliction is preparing us for something greater—an eternal weight of glory. Remember that eternity does exist and that our time here is only momentary—a blip in the great story that's being written for eternity.

4. Eagerly wait. Look forward to the redemption of our bodies and to our union with the Savior. We have great hope, and this hope allows us to wait with gratitude for what the Lord has prepared for us. Nothing will compare to the perfection of heaven. Nothing can come close. Our minds can't grasp what it will be like to no longer mourn or weep and instead to delight and rejoice forever. And to be without sin—yes! We will be without sin! The daily battle we face with our flesh will be over. Let's fix our eyes on him as we anticipate that good gift we will receive one day: eternal life and everlasting enjoyment.

When I daydream about the glories of heaven, I imagine asking the Lord a multitude of questions about the Bible that I didn't quite understand. I think he'll clear up some of our controversies, and won't that be nice! I think of sitting across the table at a feast with people from every tribe, tongue, and nation. There will be people groups who hated one another dining together, and I'll ask them to pass the salmon covered in capers and lemon and dill and freshly cut fruit. I'll eat bread with lots of butter because cholesterol is something we won't need to worry about. I'll high-five that friend who was an enemy, and then I'll go hang out with the apostle Paul, because it's Paul, y'all! I won't be sorrowful but always rejoicing. I'll just be rejoicing. Awesome!

Take a moment to imagine what it will be like, and consider how that may help you to endure. I think the psalmist would imagine the beauty, perfection, and loveliness of being with God for eternity:

> You make known to me the path of life;
>> in your presence there is fullness of joy;
>> at your right hand are pleasures forevermore. (Ps 16:11)

Give yourself permission to do likewise. This isn't escapism. It's a good and right focus on what we ought to fix our eyes on every single day (2 Cor 4:18). Enjoy it. Sit in it. One day you and I will be there for eternity. God is making all things new, and all the wrong and bad will return to the original state. We will join him in saying, "It is good."

TO ENDURE TODAY, LOOK TO THE SON

In this life, we're being made more like Christ. One day, we'll be face to face with our Savior. So we press on toward the goal to win the prize. One prize—and likely the greatest—is being in perfect fellowship with Jesus forever (Phil 3:14).

I recently shared on social media a brief takeaway from a conversation I had with my mother. In our social-media world, the use of the term *blessed* has been turned into a proclamation of all the good things we have—from vacations to cars to a new home. It's often turned into a hashtag that says without saying, "I'm living my best life now." In other words, it's all about us, what we are receiving materially. But these gifts that will one day vanish are not truly about the Lord.

Blessed are those who live with God in heaven (noun) and are made holy (adjective). Blessed can also mean "happy." But for now I pray that what I shared on social media from my conversation with my mom will encourage you to think of all God's blessings in your life (Ps 103). Mom wrote, "People talk about being blessed, but I know I'm blessed." She has experienced the death of her young daughter, the death of her oldest daughter, and the death of her husband. She has one kidney and has had cancer. She knows Jesus, and that's why she proclaims, "I'm blessed."

The Christian life can be lived in valleys and on mountaintops, but it's mostly walked out on the plains. Most of our days are spent in the mundane, the ordinary, the routine. Such monotony can produce complacency or apathy toward the Lord. He can become yet another thing on our to-do list rather than the delight and joy of our existence.

You and I are prone to forget the greatest love in the world. It's a love we can't fully comprehend or imagine, and yet, practically, we forget that he loves us, he pursues us, and we are his. As Robert Robinson put it in his great hymn "Come Thou Fount," we are "prone to wander, Lord, I feel it."[2]

Each day and each hour brings a fight to remember our greatest love in the world. One way for us to fight our temptation to wander toward lesser things and not to run the race set before us is to remember the love and pursuit of God. The love and the pursuit of any human pales in comparison to the love and pursuit of God.

GOD'S PURSUIT OF US

If there's an ocean of grace available to us—and there is—we find much of it proclaimed by the apostle Paul in the opening of Ephesians. In the original Greek, Ephesians 1:3-14 is one long sentence—and for good reason! Paul was astounded by the goodness of God to sinful people. We did not pursue God; he pursued us. And we would never be able to imagine, let alone earn, the spiritual blessings that the Lord bestows on us: redemption through the blood of Christ, forgiveness of sin, adoption as sons, everlasting love, an imperishable inheritance, grace upon grace, and so much more.

At least seven times, Paul referenced God's pursuit of us in this chunk of Scripture. The opening praise sets the stage: "Blessed be the God and Father of our Lord Jesus Christ, who has blessed us in Christ with every spiritual blessing" (Eph 1:3). All the promises of God are yes and amen in Christ (2 Cor 1:20). God withholds only those things that are not for your absolute best.

There's only one person qualified to give us access to these spiritual blessings: Jesus Christ. Paul mentioned him at least fifteen times in the first fourteen verses of Ephesians. He reminded us later in Ephesians that our salvation is not our own doing; it is a gift of God *in* Christ Jesus (Eph 2:4-9). In Christ and because of Christ, we have the gift of redemption and all that comes with that amazing gift. The cosmic reality of our union with Christ is worthy of our every praise.

So, what are these blessings? The verses that follow verse three tell us.

God *chose* us before the foundation of the world (Eph 1:4). When we think about a mountain like Everest or a sea like the Mediterranean, we should join in the song of the psalmist:

> When I look at your heavens, the work of your fingers,
>> the moon and the stars, which you have set in place,
> what is man that you are mindful of him,
>> and the son of man that you care for him? (Ps 8:3-4)

God set the world in motion. The sky proclaims his awesomeness; creation points to his holiness. And yet he is mindful of sinful people? Yes! Before he created the heavens, he chose you. Our holy, majestic, awesome God was mindful of us. He wasn't surprised when Adam and Eve sinned. He knew that one day we'd fall and that we would continually sin against him. Still he chose us. God's character is just, holy, and oh so merciful.

Paul went on to write that Jesus has also secured our *right-eousness*, and we will one day be presented as blameless before the Father (Eph 1:4). Jesus accomplished something we could never do on our own. To be blameless is to be free from guilt, free from all blame. No one walking this earth is blameless. We have all sinned and fall short of the glory of God (Rom 3:23). Yet in Christ we are indeed blameless. Our sins are forgiven and washed away. In Christ we will be presented as blameless on the final day. Even now Jesus is interceding for us. We are covered with his righteousness.

In Christ, we are infinitely *loved*. God has bestowed spiritual blessings on us out of his love for us. God's love is incomprehensible; we can't fathom it. When we try to compare our love to God's love, we see that we fall awfully short. God *is* love (1 Jn 4:8). Everything we know about God and every action we see from God is bound up in his love. God cannot act apart from his love.

The greatest display of God's love is through the blood of Christ: "In this is love, not that we have loved God but that he loved us and sent his Son to be the propitiation for our sins"(1 Jn 4:10). This is a love that we could never fully understand with our finite minds and limited ability to extend love. God's love is incomparable, and it's reserved for you in Christ.

God could have stopped there, but he didn't. If we are in Christ, we are also *adopted* sons and daughters of God (Eph 1:5). This is an inseparable adoption (Rom 8:35-39). As Christians, we are God's children, heirs of all he has (Rom 8:32)—fellow heirs with Christ (Rom 8:16-17).

Before the foundation of the world, God had us in mind and determined to create us and then adopt us as his very own children. We get to approach our majestic God boldly (Heb 4:16) as our Abba Father (Rom 8:15). There is nothing sweeter than to know that we are secure, safe, and loved by God in such an intimate way. In Christ, we have open access to our almighty heavenly Father.

MORE THAN WE CAN IMAGINE

The riches of what it means to be in Christ are far greater than anything we could ask or imagine. We've only scratched the surface! God chose us, predestined us, adopted us, and lavished us with grace and with an inheritance beyond our wildest dreams—all to the praise of his glory.

When we're tempted to think that we must somehow be good enough to deserve God's love, we need to bathe in Ephesians 1:3-14. These verses tell us a different story—a *much* better one. The God of the universe thought of us, created us, sought us out, sent his Son to die for us, and forgave us. We don't do anything but *receive* it.

Remembering these great truths helps us fight for the endurance that he has bought for us. He has already promised to finish this work. He has given us everything we need and more.

Keep running the race set before you. Remember his love that makes us eager to know him, to love and obey him, not because of anything we can earn but because of all that he has done. Because he first pursued us, we can pursue him with sacred endurance.[3]

ACKNOWLEDGMENTS

As you likely know, most books aren't truly done without a wonderful posse of people. *Sacred Endurance* is no different.

First, this book is dedicated to my best and most faithful friend. He is also my husband. Thern: thank you for holding my hand through this process. Over the past few years we've had to learn to endure various trials and God has been so faithful. Your steady faith and consistent love has been the anchor this family needs. Your love for me is something I am overwhelmed by daily. Every day with you is more special than the last. I love you and love this life with you.

Thank you also, Weston and Sydney. I can't believe I get to be your mother. I pray that you would know and love this Lord that promises to finish the good work he began in you. I love you dearly.

Thank you to my agent Don Gates who has been a source of encouragement and support. You are a gift! Thank you to my editor extraordinaire, Al Hsu. We joked about me needing to endure to get this book completed. Thank you for your patience with me and your consistent encouragement and wisdom throughout the process. Grateful for the marketing team and all involved in getting this book to those who might benefit from it, specifically, Christina Gilliland, Alisse Goldsmith-Wissman, Krista Clayton, and the entire team at IVP.

Thank you to the ERLC Team. I work with gems who are always a source of encouragement through writing. Thank you to Andrew Walker, Randy Alcorn, Ray and Jani Ortlund, Tom and Linda Strode, Paul and Sandy Cochran, and so many others who took time to allow me to share their stories in this book or on my site. Thank you to Chris Martin who is such a faithful friend and allows me to bounce things off him even though he works for a different publisher! Melissa, Jen, Courtney, Kristie, Catherine, Jenn, and a number of other wonderful friends—thank you! Thank you to my pastor, Jed— seriously grateful for you.

God has been so faithful to give me friends and family to help get this book in the hands of others. This is what enduring looks like—hand in hand with others. Thank you for walking with me.

And, my dearest Lord, thank you for always being faithful to me. You are the reason I write, and I pray it is glorifying and pleasing to you.

Appendix

WHAT ABOUT THOSE WHO DON'T ENDURE TO THE END?

I would be doing you a disservice if I didn't address the elephant in the room. The fact is, some won't endure to the end. Some who proclaim Jesus will leave the faith, deny God's existence altogether, or begin to believe teachings contrary to the elementary knowledge of the Savior. Some would ask if that person was ever really a true Christian. Because we can't know that for certain, I will focus on the helpful warnings we see in Hebrews 5:11–6:12.

The problem the writer of Hebrews is writing about has been labeled apostasy, which is the abandonment or renunciation of a religious belief. The goal in exploring these texts isn't to scare us or cause doubt of our salvation but rather so we may not be sluggish in our faith and so that we would have full assurance.

The readers at that time had become dull of hearing and sluggish (Heb 5:11; 6:12). They were immature in their faith and needed, as the writer of Hebrews explained, milk and not solid food. Solid food (that is, in-depth teaching) is for the mature, and they were not ready for it (Heb 6:12). In the previous verses the author was attempting to explain Jesus' priesthood. Because he knew that the reader wouldn't understand, he paused and inserted the section we're now exploring.

It isn't that they were intellectually inferior; it's that they didn't want to learn. Essentially they were being lazy. They were sluggish in the most literal sense. It says that they could have been teachers at that point but had to relearn elementary truths. Although the text doesn't explain what exactly they were doing or how they were doing it, I do think that laziness in the faith may have led them to being enticed by other teachings. Paul warned the Galatians about deserting him, who called them in the grace of Christ, and turning to a different gospel (Gal 1:6-10). We also see in Colossians Paul's warnings about being captive to philosophy and empty deceit, according to human tradition and not according to Christ (Col 2:8).

Hebrews isn't addressing an arrival at knowing all things, and we'll never arrive or grow out of the need to learn anyway. This is about progress and growing. At some point we should progress past simple truth because of a desire in our hearts to know our Savior. The writer of Hebrews was teaching a greater understanding of Jesus as a high priest (Heb 5:1-10). I imagine he wasn't expecting his readers to understand everything, or he wouldn't be teaching it! But I suspect they may not have understood the basic outworkings of Jesus as the Great High Priest (Heb 2:17; 4:14).

I don't think that means they needed to understand, for example, the full context of Genesis 14, the Day of Atonement, or the actions of the Levitical priests—at least not fully. But they would need to understand that Jesus was the ultimate sacrifice for their and our sins, Jesus is greater than any priest, and Jesus has made a way to the Father. The hope is that we'd understand that basic truth and walk it out in faith with the goal of learning more and more that leads to worship and devotion.

This knowledge helps guard us from error. As theologian and professor Thomas Schreiner explains in his commentary on Hebrews:

> Spiritual maturity, the author teaches, doesn't depend fundamentally on intellectual ability. It isn't correlated with theological depth or the ability to grasp theological truths. The readers were spiritual infants because they weren't putting into practice what they had learned. They needed to be instructed in the fundamentals of the faith because they hadn't progressed on to spiritual maturity.[1]

We see the seriousness of the issue in Hebrews 6:4-8, which is interpreted in various ways. Many biblical scholars would disagree on what it means.

> For it is impossible, in the case of those who have once been enlightened, who have tasted the heavenly gift, and have shared in the Holy Spirit, and have tasted the goodness of the word of God and the powers of the age to come, and then have fallen away, to restore them again to repentance, since they are crucifying once again the Son of God to their own harm and holding him up to contempt. For land that has drunk the rain that often falls on it, and produces a crop useful to those for whose sake it is cultivated, receives a blessing from God. But if

it bears thorns and thistles, it is worthless and near to being cursed, and its end is to be burned. (Heb 6:4-8 ESV)

The confusion is whether or not the people described here were once true Christians, because they were once "enlightened," "tasted the heavenly gift," and "shared in the Holy Spirit." This does sound like people who knew Jesus. But if that's the case, "for it is impossible . . . to restore them again to repentance" does not seem to hold up with much of what the Scriptures teach about the nature of repentance (1 Jn 1:9, for example). And then the mention of thorns and thistles leads me to wonder if regeneration had ever occurred. It would seem that someone that hardened wouldn't have been a Christian to begin with. Yet I do know we can be tempted to forget and abandon the truth. So, although there's confusion here, the warning is still valid, and we should all be careful that we don't fall (1 Cor 10:12).

Why is this even important? Because the wrath of God is real, and we need a healthy fear of the Lord. God's wrath is not irrational, impulsive, or immoral. As J. I. Packer wrote in *Knowing God:* "God's love, as the Bible views it, never leads him to foolish, impulsive, immoral actions in the way that its human counterpart too often leads us. And in the same way, God's wrath in the Bible is never the capricious, self-indulgent, irritable, morally ignoble thing that human anger so often is."[2]

The wrath of God is a way God delivers or administers his justice. It is not cruel; rather it is God's righteous judgment (Rom 2:5-6). But we aren't used to thinking in this way. We don't want to consider God's wrath. We want to ignore Romans 1:18:

"The wrath of God is revealed from heaven against all ungodliness and unrighteousness of men, who by their unrighteousness suppress the truth." Why would Jesus, speaking to crowds, reference a "wrath to come" (Luke 3:7)? As a matter of fact, why would the Lord include wrath in the Bible at all if it wasn't something that we needed to know and learn about, according to his character? God is holy and just, and sin can't be in his presence. That's why we say, "Thank you, Jesus." He satisfied the wrath we deserve, for it is Jesus who delivers us from the wrath to come (1 Thess 1:10).

Packer added, "If we would know God, it is vital that we face the truth concerning his wrath, however unfashionable it may be, and however strong our initial prejudices against it. Otherwise we shall not understand the gospel of salvation from wrath, nor the propitiatory achievement of the cross, nor the wonder of the redeeming love of God."[3]

As we meditate on this characteristic of God's wrath and as we fully understand what Jesus did as a result, we can't help but worship. Amazing grace takes on a whole new meaning when we consider what that grace cost. Our gratitude for his forgiveness and God's sacrifice grows stronger—as does our reverence. The wrath of God causes us to stand in awe of God and leads us to obedience. Our obedience isn't because we're afraid of God; it's because we love him so much, the overflow of our thanksgiving leads us to submit gladly to him.

So we don't need to live in fear of apostasy! But we do need to heed the warnings. Here are some questions to help us diagnose whether or not we're veering off the road:

- Am I drifting away from the truth of the gospel?

- Am I more interested in the world and all it has to offer than in the Lord?

- Do I find myself being taken in by philosophies that oppose basic Christian doctrine?

- Have I withdrawn from the church and activities related to church and the Christian life?

If your answer is yes to any or all of these questions and it doesn't alarm you, perhaps you should pray for the Lord to give you an eagerness for him. Also consider meeting with someone who may be able to listen and help you diagnose what you're battling.

Chances are, if you answered yes to any of those questions, you aren't satisfied with the state of your soul or your walk. Praise God! Ask for help. I believe wholeheartedly that the promise found in Philippians is true for all his redeemed: "And I am sure of this, that he who began a good work in you will bring it to completion at the day of Jesus Christ" (Phil 1:6).

DISCUSSION QUESTIONS

1. CALLED TO A RACE

1. Can you recall a time in your life where a hardship threatened to overtake you? What helped you to persevere through it?

2. Trillia talks about the race of the Christian life alternating between times of effortlessness and then exhaustion. What part of the race are you in right now?

3. What truth about God are you most tempted to doubt when you are in a trial? What truth has most strengthened you?

4. Trillia discusses the endurance it takes to keep going in our race. She also says we don't finish our race in our own strength but absolutely need God's power to endure. Which of these two thoughts do you need to most remember right now and why?

5. Can you think of any stories, either in the Old or New Testament, that illustrate both the endurance of God's people and God's power to sustain to the end?

2. JESUS AND THE CLOUD OF WITNESSES

1. As Trillia writes about the great "cloud of witnesses" from Hebrews 12, name the ways you might be inspired and motivated by their cheering for us. What might you say

to those who feel discouraged at the thought of all those witnesses?

2. As we think through the comparison between a Christian and an athlete who must strip off all but the most needed clothing for the sake of victory, describe a time where you had to dramatically throw off a sin that entangled you.

3. In 1 Corinthians 10:13, it says that God always provides a way of escape when temptations come our way. How have you seen God's provision of an escape route when you've been tempted? If you can, share a current temptation for which you are presently searching for a way of escape.

4. How has condemnation specifically affected your growth in godliness? What has been your favorite remedy against condemnation?

5. Can you think of any examples of people who have joined the "cloud of witnesses" (whether from the Bible or loved ones now with the Lord) who fixed their eyes on Jesus until the end? Describe the way they affect your own faith and endurance.

3. THE RIGHT MOTIVATIONS

1. Hebrews 12:2 says that Jesus endured and obeyed for the joy set before him. Describe particular joys set before you that God uses to empower you to persevere.

2. Trillia says, "Running with the wrong motivations . . . leaves us depleted and wanting to give up this race." Have you ever experienced this? Share if you can.

3. How have you personally discerned when your motivations

have shifted to one of self-glory rather than for God's glory?

4. What has been helpful/unhelpful for you in handling wrong motivations?

5. Paul says that it's the love of Christ that compels (2 Corinthians 5:14). Describe a time in your life when you were living compelled by his love, whether in the past or present.

4. THE REAL CHRISTIAN LIFE

1. Are you most apt to stumble into the pitfalls of the prosperity gospel, have superstitious fear of disaster, or throw out faith in God's promises altogether?

2. Think of the most wonderful strengths God has given you. Consider how many of them were worked into you through suffering.

3. Which truth do you most need to hear right now: that suffering in this life shouldn't be a surprise, or that he promises joy and reward in the suffering?

4. What story from either the Old Testament or New Testament can you think of that highlights both God's sovereignty and goodness?

5. Trillia talks about the importance of letting ourselves mourn when suffering comes. She also talks about how vital it is to face our trials with faith in God to sustain us. Can you think of a time when you were able to both mourn and, at some point (whether through the mourning or afterward), stand in faith on God's promises?

5. ENDURING AND THE MIND

1. Consider two of the major threats to endurance that Trillia mentioned: cynicism and complacency. Do either of those currently seem to be a threat to you? What might it look like for you to move in the opposite direction, toward faith?

2. We know that we will be transformed by the renewing of our minds as we put our hope in God's promises. Which of God's promises do you and the people in your life need to be renewed by?

3. What are the "things above" that you have set your mind on that have helped you endure in your faith?

4. Have you ever experienced rejoicing in suffering? What did that look like?

5. Paul saw his loss of prestige in society as a gain because he would rather have righteousness through Christ than impressive outward actions. Have you, like Paul, ever lost something the world values that led to gaining more of God?

6. ENDURING IN SOCIETY AND THE WORLD

1. Trillia talks about many different troubles in the world and society in this chapter. Which trouble most affects your race in this life?

2. What does it look like in your life when you stop and take a break from carrying your burdens and take captive your thoughts?

3. As far as you're able to tell, how have you seen Satan's

attacks combine with human sin to try to come against God and his people?

4. How should we fight back against Satan, who prowls around seeking opportunities to devour, with the far superior power of God?

5. Can you describe a time where God has been a refuge and strength for you in a time of trouble?

7. THE HEART NEEDED, THE STRENGTH SUPPLIED

1. When do you find your desire for God comes naturally? When is it more of a struggle?

2. Have you ever experienced a growing desire for God as you've preached truth and encouragement to your own soul? What was that like?

3. In what ways have you been aware that you were/are abiding in Christ?

4. Describe a time where you've struggled to hold on to Christ, but you knew he was securely holding on to you.

5. What do you most need to preach to yourself right now, minute by minute?

8. TAKING STEPS IN PRACTICAL DISCIPLINES

1. In 1 Corinthians 9:25, it talks about how we will gain an imperishable prize when our race is over. What perishable prizes might you be tempted to run for in moments of distraction or confusion?

2. What area of your life currently gets the most intentional attention and self-discipline? Describe the result of your

devotion, planning, and focus in this area. How might this inspire you in the spiritual disciplines?

3. Trillia says spiritual disciplines "most definitely aren't the way to gain a seat at the Lord's table. They're meant to help us finish well and enjoy the Lord." Can you think of a person in Scripture who ran their race to finish well and enjoyed the Lord in the process?

4. In response to this chapter's call for honest and consistent prayer, consider which of these two is most difficult for you.

5. Share a time when either fasting or solitude has been used by God to prepare you for something or give you strength.

9. BROKEN AND CONTRITE

1. Why do you think the word "sin" isn't mentioned in some Christian circles? Is it an awkward word for you to talk about? Why or why not?

2. Which aspect of God's character do you need to most be reminded of right now—his powerful sovereignty or his love?

3. If we have repented of our sins and are now living for Jesus, why do you think we are asked to continue repenting over sin?

4. Can you think of a time in your life where repentance gave you a sense of walking in the light as God lifted your burden?

5. In what way does it encourage you that we are made in the image of God?

DISCUSSION QUESTIONS

10. DON'T GO IT ALONE

1. If you have been a regular member of a church, what was/ is your greatest joy of living life in a church community?

2. If Jesus loved the church enough to die for it, how can we practically love the church as well?

3. What hinders you from seeking discipleship?

4. Think of a situation in Scripture or in your own life where the love and power of God was able to overcome a rift between people.

5. How can we contribute to making our churches more like the family God has said that we are?

11. FALLING AND GETTING UP

1. Why do you think it took Nathan's involvement before David repented?

2. What lies circulate in your head when you are tempted not to get back up?

3. Would you consider yourself a bruised reed? How has God used your bruising for beauty, as he did in both David's and Peter's lives?

4. Are there any consequences of sin in your life that you have previously considered God's wrath on you? How does it change the way you think of God to know that if you are a Christian, you won't receive his wrath?

5. Has condemnation hindered you from rising up from shame? What truths should be repeated in your mind to combat the condemning thoughts?

12. LOOKING TO THE PRIZE

1. What part of our promised heavenly reward most excites you?

2. Trillia lists four ways to help fix our eyes on eternity (preach the gospel to yourself, fight idolatry, remember time, and eagerly wait). Which of those four most speaks to you as a practical step you'd like to start taking?

3. Does your view of heaven give you endurance? Why or why not?

4. Can you share a testimony of someone (either yourself or a dear one) who is aware of all that they're blessed with in the love of Jesus, in spite of not being "blessed" by the way the world defines it?

5. God's blessings in the love of Jesus include the following four (just for starters): we are chosen, we are declared righteous, we are loved, and we are adopted. Which blessing do you most need to think on right now?

NOTES

1 Called to a Race

[1]Clara Ward, "How I Got Over," 1951. Sung by Mahalia Jackson, Apollo Records.

[2]Mahlia Jackson: The Queen of the Gospel, "Final Years," www.mahaliajackson .us/biography/1969.

[3]Thomas R. Schreiner and Ardel B. Caneday, *The Race Set Before Us: A Biblical Theology of Perseverance and Assurance* (Downers Grove, IL: InterVarsity Press, 2001), 40.

2 Jesus and the Cloud of Witnesses

[1]Frederick W. Danker, Walter Bauer, William F. Arndt, and F. Wilbur Gingrich, *Greek-English Lexicon of the New Testament and Other Early Christian Literature,* 3rd ed. (Chicago: University of Chicago Press, 2000).

[2]"When he says *we are surrounded by so great a cloud of witnesses,* he assumes that Christians are aware of the presence of these spectators. The word used here for witness (*martyrs*) does not usually denote 'spectator', and yet the use of the imagery here presupposes such a meaning. Nevertheless the word which the writer has chosen tells us something about the character of the spectators. They are to be distinguished from the fickle approach of those whose only desire is to be entertained. These witnesses who watch from the stands are those well qualified to inspire – they bear witness to the faithfulness of God in sustaining them." Donald Guthrie, *Hebrews: An Introduction and Commentary*, Tyndale New Testament Commentaries (Downers Grove, IL: InterVarsity Press, 1983) 249-50.

[3]Precept Austin, "Hebrews 12 Resources," www.preceptaustin.org/hebrews _12_resources. Also, Desiring God, "Can Loved Ones in Heaven Look

Down On Me?," www.desiringgod.org/interviews/can-loved-ones-in
-heaven-look-down-on-me.

[4]The author of Hebrews does not name himself.

[5]Elder D. J. Ward, "Jesus Paid It All," Trillia Newbell, May 7, 2017, www
.trillianewbell.com/tag/elder-d-j-ward/.

[6]Philip Edgcumbe Hughes, *A Commentary on the Epistle to the Hebrews*
(Charlotte, NC: William B. Eerdmans, 1977), 522.

[7]Hughes, *A Commentary*.

3 THE RIGHT MOTIVATIONS

[1]A portion of this text was adapted from Trillia Newbell, "Sorrowful,
Yet Always Rejoicing," Desiring God, December 6, 2012, www.desiringgod
.org/articles/sorrowful-yet-always-rejoicing.

[2]A portion of this text was adapted from Trillia Newbell, "Legalism or Love?
Religious or Radical?" Desiring God, May 22, 2013, www.desiringgod
.org/articles/legalism-or-love-religious-or-radical.

[3]A portion of this text was adapted from Trillia Newbell, "Even Grace Can
Lead to Legalism," Desiring God, June 14, 2016, www.desiringgod.org
/articles/even-grace-can-lead-to-legalism.

4 THE REAL CHRISTIAN LIFE

[1]Joni Eareckson Tada, *Joni* (Grand Rapids: Zondervan, 1976).

[2]Albert Y. Hsu, *Grieving a Suicide* (Downers Grove, IL: InterVarsity Press,
2017), 48.

[3]C. S. Lewis, *Mere Christianity* (London: William Collins, 2017, 1944), 55-56.

[4]J. I. Packer, *Knowing God* (Downers Grove, IL: InterVarsity Press, 2001), 259.

[5]Randy Alcorn, interview by Trillia Newbell, May 8, 2018.

5 ENDURING AND THE MIND

[1]Allison Van Dusen, "Inside the Endurance Athlete's Mind," *Forbes*, September 22, 2008, www.forbes.com/2008/09/22/endurance-race-training
-forbeslife-cx_avd_0922sports.html#65b76f6f4711.

[2]"How Does the Brain Work?," National Center for Biotechnology Information, www.ncbi.nlm.nih.gov/books/NBK279302.

[3]Oxford Living Dictionary, s.v. "cynicism," accessed June 5, 2019, https://
en.oxforddictionaries.com/definition/cynicism.

[4]Marilynne Robinson, *The Death of Adam: Essays on Modern Thought* (New
York: Picador, 2014), 78.

[5]Oxford Living Dictionary, s.v. "complacency," accessed June 5, 2019, https://en.oxforddictionaries.com/definition/complacency.

[6]Thomas Chalmers, "The Expulsive Power of a New Affection," Mongerism, www.monergism.com/thethreshold/sdg/Chalmers,%20Thomas %20-%20The%20Expulsive%20Power%20of%20a%20New%20Af.pdf.

[7]R. C. Sproul, "Renewing Your Mind," Ligonier Ministries, www.ligonier .org/learn/devotionals/renewing-your-mind/.

6 ENDURING IN SOCIETY AND THE WORLD

[1]See my *United: Captured by God's Vision for Diversity* (Chicago: Moody, 2014) in which I share more about my story.

[2]Portions of this text are adapted from Trillia Newbell, "Fighting Our Fears with God-Given Faith," *Christianity Today*, www.christianitytoday.com /edstetzer/2015/june/fighting-our-fears-with-god-given-faith.html.

[3]Anthony J. Carter, *Blood Work* (Orlando, FL: Reformation Trust, 2013), 19.

[4]Trillia Newbell, "More than a Month Long," February 6, 2017, transcription of an interview with John Perkins, www.trillianewbell.com /2017/02/06/more-than-a-month-long.

[5]John Perkins, *One Blood: Parting Words to the Church on Race* (Chicago: Moody, 2018).

7 THE HEART NEEDED, THE STRENGTH SUPPLIED

[1]A portion of this section was adapted from Trillia Newbell, "Learning to Abide," Desiring God, June 10, 2014, www.desiringgod.org/articles /learning-to-abide-in-christ.

[2]Sister Kelly, "Proud of the 'Ole Time' Religion," in Milton C. Sernett, ed., *African American Religious History* (Durham, NC: Duke University Press, 1999), 73.

8 TAKING STEPS IN PRACTICAL DISCIPLINES

[1]Robert Weisman, "Most Americans Still Do Not Work Out Enough," *Boston Globe*, April 14, 2013, www.bostonglobe.com/business/2013/04/13 /exercise-goals-are-increasing-but-most-americans-still-not-work-out -enough/3P6M8aLmTxQNTeZtynhglM/story.html.

[2]This section was adapted from Trillia Newbell, "The Spiritual Gift of Physical Exercise," *Christianity Today,* October 5, 2015, www.christianitytoday.com /women/2015/october/spiritual-gift-of-physical-exercise.html.

[3]Conrad Mbewe, *Foundations for the Flock* (Hannibal, MO: Granted Ministries Press, 2011), Kindle loc. 389.

9 Broken and Contrite

[1]Augustine, *Confessions*, trans. Henry Chadwick (Oxford: Oxford University Press, 2009), 32.

10 Don't Go It Alone

[1]This section was adapted from Trillia Newbell, "When You Don't Love the Church," *Tabletalk Magazine*, September 4, 2017, https://tabletalkmagazine.com/posts/2017/09/dont-love-church.

[2]A portion of this text was adapted from Trillia Newbell, "Three Benefits of Discipleship," Desiring God, February 13, 2014, www.desiringgod.org/articles/three-benefits-of-discipleship.

[3]A portion of this text was adapted from Trillia Newbell, "Why Accountability Matters," Desiring God, March 19, 2013, www.desiringgod.org/articles/why-accountability-matters.

[4]Natasha Sistrunk Robinson, *A Sojourner's Truth* (Downers Grove, IL: InterVarsity Press, 2018), 133.

[5]A portion of this section was taken from Trillia Newbell, "How Miscarriage Led to My Crisis of Faith," *Christianity Today*, April 8, 2015, www.christianitytoday.com/ct/2015/april-web-only/losing-baby-not-losing-my-faith.html.

11 Falling and Getting Up

[1]It could be argued that David raped Bathsheba, which is increasingly becoming the interpretation of the text, although not held by all scholars.

[2]John Newton, "Thoughts upon the African Slave Trade," Bible Study Tools, www.biblestudytools.com/classics/newton-posthumous-works/thoughts-upon-the-african-slave-trade.html.

[3]John Newton, "Amazing Grace," Hymnal.net, www.hymnal.net/en/hymn/h/313.

12 Looking to the Prize

[1]Corrie ten Boom, *The Hiding Place* (Minneapolis: Chosen, 1971).

[2]Robert Robinson, "Come Thou Fount," Hymnal.net, www.hymnal.net/en/hymn/h/319.

[3]A portion of this text was adapted from Trillia Newbell, "The Breathtaking Love We Tend to Forget," Desiring God, February 7, 2019, www.desiringgod.org/articles/the-breathtaking-love-we-tend-to-forget.

Appendix: What About Those Who Don't Endure to the End?

[1]Thomas R. Schreiner, *Biblical Theology for Christian Proclamation: Commentary on Hebrews* (Nashville, TN: Holman Reference, 2015), 173.

[2]J. I. Packer, *Knowing God*, (Downers Grove, IL: InterVarsity Press, 2001), 151.

[3]Packer, *Knowing God*, 156.

ABOUT THE AUTHOR

Trillia J. Newbell is the author of the kids' book *God's Very Good Idea* and the Bible study *If God Is for Us* as well as the books *Enjoy: Finding the Freedom to Delight Daily in God's Good Gifts*, *Fear and Faith: Finding the Peace Your Heart Craves*, and *United: Captured by God's Vision for Diversity*.

Her writing on issues of faith, family, and diversity has been published in the *Knoxville News-Sentinel*, Desiring God, True Woman, *Christianity Today*, The Gospel Coalition, and more. She is a commentator for World Radio (the sister platform of *World Magazine*). She has spoken at numerous conferences, churches, women's retreats, colleges, and seminaries, including True Woman, The Gospel Coalition women's conference, Southeastern Theological Seminary, and more. She is the director of community outreach for the Ethics and Religious Liberty Commission for the Southern Baptist Convention.

Her greatest love besides God is her family. She is married to her best friend and love, Thern. They reside with their two children near Nashville.

trillianewbell.com
facebook.com/TrilliaNewbell
twitter.com/trillianewbell
instagram.com/trillianewbell